Nineteenth-Century Italian Women Writers and the Woman Question

Nineteenth-Century Italian Women Writers and the Woman Question focuses on the literary, journalistic and epistolary production of the Italian woman writer Neera, pseudonym for Anna Radius Zuccari, one of the most prolific and successful women writers of late nineteenth-century Italy. This study proposes to bring Neera out of the shadows of literary marginality to which she has long been confined by analyzing her contribution to literary and cultural debates as testimony to the pivotal role she played in the creation of a female literary voice within the Italian fin-de-siècle context. Drawing from the Anglo-American feminist critical tradition; modern Italian feminist theory on the maternal order and sexual difference; and a close reading of Neera's literary, theoretical and epistolary writings, this volume examines Neera's work from a three-pronged perspective: as promoter of a maternal order in contrast to the existent paternal order, as one of few women writers to participate actively in Italy's *verismo* movement and as epistolary correspondent of leading representatives within fin-de-siècle Italian literary and journalistic circles. *Nineteenth-Century Italian Women Writers and the Woman Question* represents the first monographic volume in English dedicated exclusively to this important Italian woman writer, repositioning her within the Italian literary landscape and canon.

Catherine Ramsey-Portolano is Associate Professor and Director of Italian Studies and Modern Languages at The American University of Rome in Rome, Italy, where she teaches courses on Italian language, culture, literature and film. She has completed a BA (The University of Tennessee-Knoxville), MA (The University of Wisconsin-Madison), Laurea (LUMSA University-Rome) and PhD (University of Chicago), all in Italian Literature. Her books include *Performing Bodies: Female Illness in Italian Literature and Cinema (1860–1920)*, *The Future of Italian Teaching: Media, New Technologies and Multi-Disciplinary Perspectives* and *Rethinking Neera.*

Routledge Focus on Literature

The Quarrel Between Poetry and Philosophy
Perspectives Across the Humanities
John Burns, Matthew Caleb Flamm, William Gahan, and Stephanie Quinn

Nineteenth-Century Italian Women Writers and the Woman Question
The Case of Neera
Catherine Ramsey-Portolano

Nineteenth-Century Italian Women Writers and the Woman Question

The Case of Neera

Catherine Ramsey-Portolano

NEW YORK AND LONDON

First published 2021
by Routledge
52 Vanderbilt Avenue, New York, NY 10017

and by Routledge
2 Park Square, Milton Park, Abingdon, Oxon, OX14 4RN

Routledge is an imprint of the Taylor & Francis Group, an informa business

Library of Congress Cataloging-in-Publication Data
A catalog record for this title has been requested

ISBN: 978-0-367-50890-6 (hbk)
ISBN: 978-1-003-05168-8 (ebk)

Typeset in Times New Roman
by codeMantra

Contents

Preface

This book has been a long time coming! My interest in Neera began during my PhD studies at The University of Chicago, when I chose this writer as the topic of my dissertation, written under the attentive supervision of my advisor Rebecca West, whose excellent work on Italian women writers and feminist theory guided me throughout the dissertation process. During research visits to Italy, my meetings with Antonia Arslan, the curator of Neera's archive and author of numerous articles and volumes dedicated to her production, were fundamental in the early stages of my studies on Neera for gaining a better understanding of this woman writer's vast and varied production. A short time after finishing my dissertation, I decided to publish one of the chapters as an article, which resulted in the 2004 *Italica* article titled "Neera the *Verist* Woman Writer." I would like to thank *Italica* for allowing me to publish part of that article in this volume. My interest in Neera not only remained constant but grew, and although the idea of a volume dedicated exclusively to her was always in my mind, career and family engagements prevented me at that time from dedicating the appropriate attention to a revision of my dissertation into a volume. A panel dedicated to Neera that I organized and chaired at the 2008 AAIS/AATI Conference in Taormina, Italy, led to a fruitful outcome: the 2010 special issue titled *Rethinking Neera* of the journal *The Italianist*, co-edited with my colleague and friend Katharine Mitchell, another Neera enthusiast and scholar. Featuring invited contributions by the leading scholars on Neera from the USA and Europe, and the translation for the first time in English of her short story *Falena*, this volume has represented a cornerstone for criticism on Neera up to this point. A deviation from my focus on Neera led to the publication of my book *Performing Bodies: Female Illness in Italian Literature and Cinema (1860–1920)* in 2018, although this volume can also be connected back to Neera and the representation of hysteria found in her novel *Teresa.* After *Performing Bodies,* I decided the time had finally come to devote my attention to a volume on Neera. *Nineteenth-Century Italian Women Writers and the Woman Question: The Case of Neera* represents the first monographic volume in English dedicated exclusively to this important Italian woman writer, repositioning her within the Italian literary landscape and canon. The publication of this volume now is timely for today's increased attention to and appreciation of the many contributions to all fields of intellectual, artistic and cultural production by women. I would like to thank the many family members, friends, colleagues and advisors whose support, guidance and encouragement over the years have helped me achieve this long awaited goal.

Introduction

Fin-de-siècle European scientific discourse interprets women through the lens of their reproductive function in society. The works of positivist thinkers, such as Auguste Comte,[1] Cesare Lombroso[2] and Paul Julius August Moebius,[3] provide evidence for how the supremacy of the maternal instinct in the female nature excludes women's capacity for intellectual and artistic activity. In the 1893 study *La donna delinquente, la prostituta e la donna normale* (The delinquent woman, the prostitute and the normal woman), Lombroso argues that intelligence throughout the animal kingdom varies inversely based on fertility (132). Darwinian theories on women's mental and physical inferiority confirm women's role in society as mothers, permeating beyond the realm of scientific circles to influence the reception of women writers by their male counterparts. Drawing from scientific discourse,[4] fin-de-siècle Italian literary critics argue in their reviews of women's literary production that maternal functions and qualities limit women writers' potential for intellectual and creative achievement. In *La letteratura della nuova Italia* (Literature of the new Italy, 1914), for example, renowned philosopher and literary critic Benedetto Croce asserts that women are more effective at being mothers than at being writers, separating notions of female creativity into two distinct spheres, biological and artistic:

> Sembra che le donne, valenti a svolgere in sé per nove mesi un germe di vita, a partorirlo travagliosamente, ad allevarlo con un'intelligente pazienza che ha del prodigioso, siano di solito incapaci di regolari gestazioni poetiche: i loro parti artistici sono quasi sempre prematuri: anzi, alla concezione segue istantanea la *dèliverance*, e il neonato è poi gettato sulla strada, privo di tutti quegli aiuti di cui avrebbe bisogno.[5]

The contrast outlined by the leading literary critic of the day, juxtaposing women's capability as mothers against their incapability as writers, reveals how women writers of the time were evaluated in terms of their female qualities, first among which figured their maternal function. In *The Woman Writer in Late 19th Century Italy: Gender and the Formation of Literary Identity* (1992), Lucienne Kroha contextualizes Croce's literary criticism of women writers by recognizing him as the "one major critic who managed to show some enthusiasm for the new crop of women writers," while also noting that "his general attitude to these women is more than somewhat patronizing" (2). Italian women of the period struggled to overcome not only pseudo-scientific perceptions of their biological nature but also the legal restrictions which limited their realm of activity to the domestic domain. Late nineteenth-century Italian emancipationists, such as Anna Maria Mozzoni and Anna Kulis-cioff,[6] sought to bring about recognition of women's rights within Italian society, calling for equality as they demanded the right to vote and free access for women to education and professions. The literary and journalistic contributions of fin-de-siècle Italian women writers, which presented readers with the female perspective, were also influential in bringing attention to women's inferior status within society.[7]

One such woman writer was Anna Radius Zuccari (1846–918), in art Neera, a Milanese writer who addressed women's issues in her narrative, theoretical and journalistic production. Neera's prolific activity as novelist, demonstrated by the publication of 22 novels and eight volumes of short stories, together with the critical appreciation she received from esteemed literary critics of the day, confirms her status as one of the leading figures within fin-de-siècle Italian literary circles.[8] Her fame was not limited exclusively to Italy, as revealed by the categorization of Neera in the volume *La donna italiana descritta da scrittrici italiane in una serie di conferenze tenute all'Esposizione Beatrice di Firenze* (The Italian woman described by Italian women writers in a series of conferences held at the Beatrice Exposition in Florence, 1890) as one of three Italian women writers, along with Bruno Sperani and Matilde Serao, envied by France and England (Ferruggia et al. 299). In 1890, Neera was, in fact, at the peak of her literary career, her success with literary critics and public alike firmly established with the success of her novel *Teresa* in 1886.[9] By that time, many of her novels had already been, or were soon to be, translated into the major European languages.[10] Neera's narrative production was supplemented throughout her career by an equally constant and prolific non-novelistic activity, ten volumes of essays and two poetry volumes, which often provided the setting for the defense of her work, views and poetic ideal. She collaborated with the most important Italian literary journals of the period, such as *Pungolo, Fanfulla della domenica, Corriere del Mattino, Corriere di Napoli, Il Giorno, Corriere della Sera, Vita Nuova, Il Marzocco* and *Nuova Antologia*, as well as French journals such as *Revue blue* and *Journal des Débats*, publishing articles dedicated to women's issues that were collected in volumes such as *Battaglie per un'idea* (Battles for an idea, 1898) and *Le idee di una donna* (The ideas of a woman, 1903).

Regardless of her accomplishments and the success she obtained in her time, today Neera is a member of what Antonia Arslan has labelled the "submerged galaxy,"[11] referencing the many late nineteenth-century women writers now largely forgotten by critics and public alike. In "Nineteenth-Century Women Writers between Marginality and (Aspirations of) Inclusion: A Puzzling Balance" (2015), Ombretta Frau and Cristina Gragnani argue that "with very few exceptions, the nineteenth century Italian female literary corpus could be classified as nameless, since it was never acknowledged by intellectual history" (31–32). The problem for fin-de-siècle women writers, as for many women writers even today in Italy,[12] is not getting published or selling copies but getting recognition. In "'The Ferrante Effect': In Italy Women Writers are Ascendant" (2019), Anna Momigliano notes the obstacles that generations of Italian women writers have faced to have their work appreciated and recognized as worthy in a country where "women have generally been kept far from the Italian canon" and where "literary fiction has long been considered a man's game."[13]

This study proposes to bring Neera out of the shadows of literary marginality to which she has long been confined by analyzing her contribution to literary and cultural debates, demonstrating the pivotal role she played in the creation of a female literary voice within the fin-de-siècle Italian context. From a methodological standpoint, I draw from the Anglo-American feminist critical tradition, modern Italian feminist theory on the maternal order and sexual difference and a close reading of Neera's literary, theoretical and epistolary writings in order to examine this woman writer's work from a three-pronged perspective: as promoter of a maternal order in contrast to the existent paternal order, as one of few women writers to participate actively in Italy's *verismo* movement and as epistolary correspondent of leading representatives within fin-de-siècle Italian literary and journalistic circles. This study represents the first monographic volume in English dedicated exclusively to this important Italian woman writer, repositioning her within the Italian literary landscape and canon.

In Chapter 1, I discuss Neera's personal experience as a woman and writer in fin-de-siècle Italy to construct an intellectual biography of the writer. References in her autobiographical texts *Confessioni letterarie* (Literary confessions, 1891) and *Una giovinezza del secolo XIX* (A childhood in the nineteenth century, 1919) as well as from her *epistolari* (letter exchanges) provide insight into what spurred Neera to write in a period of Italian history when intellectual professions were not easily accessible to women, as well as the difficulties she faced in doing so.

Chapter 2 examines Neera's privileging of a maternal order in her narrative and theoretical writings in contrast to the paternal order of turn-of-the-century Italian society. I will analyze the evolution of the theme that dominates throughout her work: the female condition in late nineteenth-century Italian society. In the article "Il lavoro della donna" (Women's work), Neera acknowledges her dedication to studying and examining the theme of women's suffering (*Battaglie per un'idea* 65). Throughout her literary career, Neera's narrative production becomes increasingly socially engaged as her novels evolve from making women responsible for their transgressions to denouncing society's responsibility for female oppression and exhorting the possibility for female redemption and autonomy in women's maternal mission. By exalting women's unique qualities in her narrative and theoretical production, Neera proposes the feminine and the maternal as capable of liberating women from society's oppression. In his 1979 article "Madre due volte" (Twice mother), Edoardo Sanguineti argues, in fact, that in Neera's work "il mito della femminilità come mammosità è gestito come arma di classe" [the myth of femininity as motherhood is dealt with as a weapon of class] (295). Although Neera was critical of the budding feminist cause, activists of the period recognized the importance of her role as a woman writer and the contribution to the cause offered by her work.[14] By proposing an order that values the female nature and maternal role, Neera becomes a model for modern Italian feminist thought on sexual difference and the maternal order.[15] I contextualize what many critics have referred to as Neera's "two faces" by demonstrating the continuity of themes between Neera's theoretical and narrative production.[16]

Chapter 3 positions Neera within the nineteenth-century literary canon as a *verist* writer. Although her production ranges from the late romanticism of her early works to the symbolism and idealism of her later novels, the quality of Neera's work from the *verist* period and her active participation in and contribution to this literary movement confirm her rightful place within the Italian literary canon as *verist* writer. The novels *Teresa* (1886), *Lydia* (1887) and *L'indomani* (The day after, 1889), defined by Antonia Arlsan as Neera's "trittico della fanciulla" [trilogy of the young woman] (*Dame, galline e regine* 128), provide a close analysis of women's condition in turn-of-the-century Italian society by presenting stories of hysteria, neurosis and suicide brought on by experiences of spinsterhood, unfulfilled love and marital dissatisfaction. I will examine *Teresa* in the context of *verismo* and in relation to the works of other *veristi* to demonstrate that she was one of a select group of Italian writers in the years 1870–90 to attempt a renewal of Italian literature by incorporating naturalist poetics into their narrative production. In the years surrounding the publication of *Teresa*, Neera and Luigi Capuana share, through book dedications and letters, their thoughts on poetics and their opinions on the state of the Italian novel.[17] Letter exchanges between Neera and other *veristi*, such as Giovanni Verga and Federico De Roberto, further allow for positioning her as an active participant in contemporary literary debates on *verismo*. The exchange of ideas with *veristi* and the implementation of those ideas in her literary production make Neera an essential point of reference for a discussion on *verismo*, a role that is often overlooked today.

Chapter 4 examines the differing roles adopted by Neera in cultural and literary debates of the period. Her numerous epistolary exchanges with important figures within literary, artistic and journalistic circles provide an important example of a woman writer's "private" voice and facilitate a better understanding of the complex context in which fin-de-siècle women writers were active, revealing not only her prominent and influential role in Italian literary and cultural contexts but also the multi-faceted nature of these interactions. In her letters to acclaimed male writers and critics, Neera adopts the role of the uncertain woman writer seeking guidance and assurance from fatherly figures. However, in her letters to emerging male writers, Neera takes on a motherly role, providing guidance and encouragement to young artists. Neera's letter exchanges with women writers reveal a shared understanding of the difficulties of being a woman writer and point to the desire and need, in those years, for the creation of a female network of collaboration. The differing roles exhibited by Neera in her various epistolary exchanges represent this woman writer's multiple voices, adopted as required by the circumstances of the occasion. I demonstrate how the private nature of the epistolary form allowed Neera to convey opinions and sentiments that she was unable to express in public settings.

Separate Spheres in Fin-de-Siècle Italy

Neera's lengthy literary career spanned from 1876, the year her first novel *Un romanzo* (A novel) was published, to 1919, the year her posthumous autobiography *Una giovinezza del secolo XIX* was published.[18] This period of Italian history, characterized by the country's recent national unification on one end and by its involvement in World War I on the other, was marked by significant transformations within society, which brought about repercussions for women's social role. In *Women and Gender in Post-Unification Italy* (2013), Katharine Mitchell and Helena Sanson note that at Unification "the doctrine of separate spheres between the genders continued to dominate Italian society: women's place was considered to be in the private, domestic sphere, that is, in the home, devoting themselves to family life" (2). Women's legal rights were relegated within the framework of the family, considered the foundation of the social order, although the second half of the nineteenth century also witnessed the birth of the Italian women's movement, as women started to demand rights in the public sphere such as the right to vote and equal access to education and professions.[19] Legally, women were regarded as property of the male head of the household, the *capofamiglia*, whether it be the father, husband or brother. In *Storia delle donne in Occidente* (History of women in the Occident, 1991), Georges Duby and Michelle Perrot note that a husband's legal supremacy over his wife derived from her *fragilitas* (fragility) and subsequent need of protection (70). According to the 1865 Italian Family Code, married women did not have access to public schools or offices; legal authority over their own children; or the right to manage their own property or money, not even that earned from their own work. Women required their husbands' authorization in all financial and legal affairs, including marital separation. Mozzoni concludes in *La donna e i suoi rapporti sociali* (Woman and her social relationships, 1864) that "la donna, in qualunque regime coniugale, è schiava o minore. Per avere un diritto materno, ella non dovrebbe essere madre che di prole illegale, e per avere il reale possesso di sé stesso e delle cose sue mai non dovrebbe piegare il collo al giogo del matrimonio" [Woman, in any conjugal regime, is a slave or lesser being. To have a maternal right, she must be mother only to illegitimate offspring, and to have real possession of herself and her belongings she should never subjugate herself to marriage] (qtd. Graziani and Corti 25).[20]

A woman's ability to financially support herself outside the family structure was limited, given that employers were not legally required to pay women workers the same salaries as men. In 1874, Italian women were granted access to higher education (high school and university), although it would take decades before they would gain free access to professions. The 1903 Carcano Law was the first law to regulate the employment of women, although women workers between the ages of 16 and 21 were grouped together with male workers under the age of 15 in terms of ability and therefore also salary. Although the turn of the century witnessed recognition of limited rights for women, the overall legal subordination of women within the family as well as within the workplace reinforced social conceptions of women as inferior, ultimately confirming their role within the family domain.

The efforts of the Italian women's emancipation movement in the second half of the nineteenth century contributed to bringing about a gradual blurring of the previously noted "separate spheres" that traditionally regulated men's and women's roles in Italian society. Women became active in ways which only a few decades earlier would have been unthinkable. One example is the proliferation of women writers in the post-Unification period, which already at the time was linked to a sort of "awakening" among women brought about by the *Risorgimento* movement for national independence, as Gemma Ferruggia observes: "Solamente dopo il completo risveglio patriottico del 1848 la donna italiana entra davvero nel campo letterario" [only after the complete patriotic awakening of 1848 did Italian women truly enter the literary field] (292). The last 20 years of the nineteenth century witnessed a real explosion in the number of women writers, active within a variety of contexts, from novels and poetry to journalism. Neera, Matilde Serao, Grazia Deledda, Marchesa Colombi, Bruno Sperani, Carolina Invernizio, Contessa Lara, Regina di Luanto, Emma, Annie Vivanti, Luigia Codemo, Caterina Percoto, Regina di Luanto, Maria Messina and Anna Franchi were the principal women writers active in Italy in the last quarter of the nineteenth century. The increase in the same period in the number of journals directed by women and dedicated to women's issues represents another example of female activism, as women worked together to bring about an increased awareness of the subordinated female condition in society. Ann Hallamore Caesar and Gabriella Romani note in *The Printed Media in Fin-de-Siècle Italy* (2011) that "the professionalization of the figure of the writer occurred in a gendered context, meaning that not only many women became professional writers beginning in the 1870s but that the publishing world became more aware of and attentive to the female readership" (Hallamore Caesar et al. 4). The three decades following Unification witnessed, in fact, the birth of journals directed toward a female audience, such as *La donna, La Cornelia, Cordelia, L'Aurora, Il Giornale delle Donne, La Missione della Donna, La Rassegna degli Interessi Femminili, Vita Femminile, Italia Femminile* and *L'Unione.*[21] Annarita Buttafuoco suggests in *Cronache femminili* (Female Chronicles, 1988) the social and cultural importance of these journals, in that the mere act of buying and reading a newspaper offered women readers the chance to gain their own point of view and break away from the stereotype of passivity (21–22). Hallamore Caesar and Romani note further that "publishers and writers alike could no longer afford to neglect the steadily growing numbers of female readers who, however small a group they still were numerically, composed a significant portion of the emerging urban consumer society" (Hallamore Caesar et al. 4). Confirming the importance of the journal *La donna*, founded in 1868 by Gualberta Alaide Beccari, Maria Linda Odorisio and Monica Turi suggest in *Donna o cosa?* (Woman or what?, 1991) that the journal served as a national point of reference in the *questione femminile* (woman question): "*La donna* svolgeva funzioni di organizzazione e di coordinamento in un periodo in cui mancavano completamente associazioni femminili di portata nazionale, ponendosi come punto di riferimento obbligato per quante si interessavano alla questione femminile" [*La donna* played an organizational and coordinating role at a time when there was a complete lack of women's associations of national importance, positioning itself as the obligatory point of reference for those who were interested in women's issues] (20). *La donna*'s unique policy of accepting only articles written by women reflects its intention to offer an alternative to the dominant male point of view. In *The Madwoman in the Attic* (1979), Sandra Gilbert and Susan Gubar affirm the importance of writing by and for women as a vehicle for resisting the traditional male portrayal of women: "Lacking the pen/penis which would enable them similarly to refute one fiction by another, women in patriarchal societies have historically been reduced to *mere* properties, to characters and images imprisoned in male texts because generated solely… by male expectations and designs" (12). The literary and journalistic contributions of fin-de-siècle women writers constituted an essential step in providing, for male and female readers alike, the female perspective in contrast to the male perspective which had traditionally dominated literary and cultural production.

Women Writers and Male Critics

Although an increased awareness of women's social inequality characterized the second half of the nineteenth century and the period witnessed certain, albeit limited, legislative advancements regarding women's rights, it is important to note that the boom in female literary and journalistic activity also provoked negative reactions from male writers and critics, some of whom perceived it as a threat and an invasion of their sphere of activity. In *Idols of Perversity*, Bram Dijkstra (1988) argues that the attempts by fin-de-siècle women writers, often segregated in their homes and socially excluded, to break out of society's restrictive roles represented a threat to the established order, comparing the hostility they faced to a literal war engaged by their male counterparts:

> When women became increasingly resistant to men's efforts to teach them, in the name of progress and evolution, how to behave within their appointed station in civilization, men's cultural campaign to educate their mates, frustrated by women's 'inherently perverse unwillingness to conform, escalated into what can truthfully be called a war on women.' (1)

Through their literary and journalistic production, women writers expressed a female voice and perspective that many of their male counterparts found threatening not only for the competition women writers represented but also because their activity demonstrated a rejection of traditional roles which limited women's sphere of activity solely to the domestic domain.

The many negative literary reviews of women's literary production by male critics point to the initially hostile and derogatory attitude women writers confronted. Many male critics openly discredited women's ability to compete with literature by men. The *Gazzetta*

Letteraria column entitled "Perché nessuna donna fu grande poetessa" (Why no woman has ever been a great poet), which appeared regularly in 1897, is just one example of the unwillingness to accept notions of women as capable of intelligent and creative thought. By opening his 1907 study *Letteratura femminile* (Women's literature) with the query, "C'è da impensiersi, come fanno taluni, dell'invadente concorrenza della donna nella letteratura narrativa?" [Is it worth worrying about, as some do, the instrusive competition by women in fiction?] (19), Capuana addresses concerns regarding the increase in the number of women writers. The critic reassures the male literary community with a negative response to his query, offering the following justification:

> Esse mettono nella loro opera d'arte un elemento tutto proprio, la femminilità; ma niente di più.... Io poi sono convinto che nell'avvenire, nel lontano avvenire, le donne saranno quel che ora sono gli uomini; ma allora gli uomini saranno tutt'altri; e la distanza rimarrà uguale a quella di oggi. Allora gli uomini lasceranno alle donne l'occupazione di scrivere romanzi, liriche, tragedie, commedie e, se ci avranno preso gusto, poemi; ma esse – aggiungo- non creeranno nulla di nuovo, perché non ci sarà altro da creare nelle forme dell'arte. Sarà un'eterna ripetizione, fino a che non si stancheranno; cosa un po' improbabile: le donne sono ostinate. (Capuana, *Letteratura femminile* 21–22)[22]

Women, according to Capuana, were incapable of originality, and therefore their literary production, simply a repetition of themes and styles already experimented by male writers, did not pose a threat. Insisting on the feminine nature of women's writing, recognizing characteristics such as sentimentalism, weak grammatical form and repetitive usurpation of themes from the male literary canon, was a common critique advanced by male intellectuals of the time.

Many male critics presented the view that if there was something to be exalted in women writers' works, it was reflective of their ability to imitate male genius. Accordingly, regarding certain women writers who achieved literary success, it was common for male critics to attribute their success to masculine characteristics and to their ability to imitate already established male literary models. In *Letteratura femminile*, for example, Capuana affirms, regarding Matilde Serao, his "ammirazione per l'opera quasi virile della scrittrice napoletana" [sincere admiration for the almost masculine work of the Neapolitan writer] (19). In his correspondence with Neera, Capuana praises the masculine quality of her work directly to the writer herself when he writes, "Quello che più mi piace nel vostro libro è la nota maschile che vi si sente. Brava davvero!" [What I really like in your work is the masculine note that one perceives. Really good job!] (Arslan, *Capuana e Neera* 185). In *La vita e il libro* (Life and the book, 1913), writer and critic Giuseppe Antonio Borgese offers the following evaluation of women writers of his time: "Ripensate a Neera, a Grazia Deledda, a Matilde Serao, a un'altra qualunque fra le illustri romanziere italiane: sono viragini, e valgono in quanto riescono a imitare i modelli dell'arte maschile" [Think again about Neera, Grazia Deledda, Matilde Serao, about any one of the illustrious Italian women novelists: they are bottomless pits, and they are worthwhile only as far as they are able to imitate models of men's art] (*La vita e il libro. Terza Serie* 192). Confirming that women writers merely adopted and repeated literary models already exhausted by male writers, Borgese notes further:

> Quando un contenuto letterario s'è impoverito e consunto, le donne, che percepiscono sempre con ritardo i movimenti storici, se ne impadroniscono estraendolo vivo e fresco dal passato; lo riscoprono, quando i loro confratelli l'hanno già seppellito, e ne compongono in un epilogo sonoro gli elementi che stanno per disperdersi. (*La vita e il libro. Seconda serie* 169)[23]

Even decades later, in the preface to the 1942 edition of Neera's autobiography *Una giovinezza del XIX secolo*, Croce offers the following appreciation of her literary talent: "la scrittrice si dimostra pensatore virile" (*Neera* 947). Literary critics, like positivist thinkers of the late nineteenth century, identified intelligence and artistic creativity as male qualities, thereby negating the female capacity for such traits.

Recourse to scientific discourse on female mental inferiority and women's natural suitability for the roles of wife and mother was prevalent within both scientific and literary circles. In *La voce che è in lei* (The voice inside her, 1980), Giuliana Morandini identifies Neera's generation of women writers, those born between 1840 and 1860, as the generation that experienced "la crisi degli anni Ottanta e Novanta e l'inasprimento positivista che questa crisi comporta con il prevalere nei riguardi della donna di stereotipi repressivi e limitanti" [the crisis of the 1890s and 90s and the positivist exacerbation that this crisis entailed with the prevalence of repressive and limiting stereotypes towards women] (9). Literary critics of the time called upon pseudo-scientific discourse regarding female inferiority, noting also many women writers' lack of formal education, in their negative reviews of women's work. Given that the legislation of the time prohibited women's access to higher education, Neera's generation of women writers found themselves in a "catch 22" situation from which it was difficult to escape: women were proclaimed and considered naturally mentally inferior, but social and legal limitations made sure they stayed that way. Contemporary male literary critics, drawing upon theories of female mental inferiority and referencing women's lack of formal education, often relegated women writers' production to a category of its own, that of "female literature." In the essays dedicated to women writers in *La letteratura della nuova Italia*, for instance, Croce notes lack of literary preparation as a common defect, one which accounts for incorrectness and imprecision of form. Borgese prides himself on being able to distinguish "*al fiuto*" (by smell) which of two men, equal in most respects, has studied the classics and obtained a high school diploma, concluding that the second will always be superior to the first for mentality, logical balance, clarity of vision, precision of will (*La vita e il libro. Seconda Serie* 360). Given that many women writers of the period did not receive a formal education and access to higher education was not granted to women until 1874,[24] the gender implications of Borgese's assertion are evident.

The negative criticism that women writers received of their work was not limited to categorizing it as feminine or as mere emulations of work by male writers. Borgese, for example, extends his negative evaluation of women writers beyond the literary realm when he links the decadence of contemporary society to the influence of women and their maternal qualities: "Ma la nostra società tende sempre più decisamente verso il lato delle madri, abbandona via via i consigli dell'intelletto per ubbriacarsi di sentimento" [Our society tends more and more decisively towards the side of the mothers, abandoning the advice of the intellect to inebriate itself with sentiment (*La vita e il libro. Seconda* 360). Men offered society the *consigli* [advice] of their intellect, whereas women's contribution brought about the effects of a mind-altering drug that inhibits one's mental capacities. Like positivist thinkers such as Lombroso, Borgese associated the rational with men and the irrational with women, confirming the traditional dichotomy of intellect/man versus body/woman. These arguments bound women to their biological role, excluding them from being able to offer contributions of an intellectual and artistic nature.

Noting in *The Feminist Encyclopedia of Italian Literature* (1997) entry for "canon" that Italian literary culture is "decidedly less represented by contributions from women" (Russell 40), Ada Testaferri argues that "literary studies in Italy have always been articulated within a discriminatory system" (Russell 42), whether it be Pietro Bembo's Renaissance model of linguistic and stylistic purity, Francesco De Sanctis's nineteenth-century literary canon based on nationalistic ideology or, in the twentieth century, Croce's individualistic and elitist criticism of art. In her 1994 essay "Women in Italian," Rebecca West notes that "[c]ontributions by women to Italian literature and culture have not in the past gone entirely unnoticed, but they have for the most part been evaluated according to traditions and criteria that made of them 'secondary' or 'minor' in the dominant context of canonical, male-authored works" (199). The lacuna of women writers in the Italian literary canon has been recognized by numerous studies which aim to uncover and spur interest in the contribution of "forgotten" figures, such as Neera, Marchesa Colombi, Contessa Lara and Vittoria Aganoor.[25] In *Writing and Performing Female Identity in Italian Culture* (2017), Virginia Picchietti and Laura A. Salsini argue that "[t]hese studies have been invaluable to the development of the field, its acceptance by the critical establishment, and the promulgation of women's cultural voices" (5). Only by evaluating female literary production in the context in which it was written is it possible to reconstruct a complete picture of the Italian fin-de-siècle's cultural and literary *milieu* and appreciate female production from various perspectives. Mitchell suggests the following regarding Neera and other *scrittrici* of her time:

> [They] embodied the tensions and contradictions that are to be found in their writings, yet which were also embedded in the fabric of the culture and society of the time. The paradoxes and contradictions of this period in Italian history were being played out in the themes, subject matter, and narrative style of women writers' works focusing on domestic issues. (*Italian Women Writers* 110)

Analyzing Neera's production within the historical and cultural framework of the period in which she was active is crucial for interpreting the various contributions of this woman writer: as anticipator of modern feminist thought on sexual difference and the maternal, as active participant in the *verismo* movement and as communicator in her epistolary correspondence of the woman writer's multi-faceted private voice. Better understanding the career of this fin-de-siècle author promotes further appreciation of the contribution of women writers to the mainstream cultural and literary context of their time, as Arslan notes:

> La cultura femminile italiana deve essere fatta uscire dall'idea dell'eccezione e dell'anomalia rara, e deve avviarsi a una sana complementarietà di visione e di discussione, mettendo in rapporto testi maschili e femminili in modo che interagiscano tra loro, che si possano studiare gli influssi reciproci. ("La galassia salvata" 13)[26]

The rediscovery and appreciation of this "lost" generation of women writers shed light on the role of women and the transformations concerning them that occurred within Italian society at that time precisely because of women's newfound voice. Rosa Cuda suggests the need to "renegotiate so-called truths," challenging works that for centuries have been considered "neutral and unbiased and proposed to speak for all" but that deny the reality of the "other," when she notes that the "historical subject, for the most part masculine, claimed universality, but in effect, spoke of and for a world configured in his own image" (43–44). Offering the female perspective, as Neera did in her literary and theoretical works, meant proposing a whole new, previously unconsidered and undervalued, worldview, one in which women could be agents of change instead of passive observers.

Bibliography of Neera's Works[27]

Novels

Addio! 1877. Milan, Baldini & Castoldi, 1919.
Anima sola. 1894. Milan, Baldini & Castoldi, 1919.
Crepuscoli di libertà. 1916. Reggio Emilia, Città armoniosa, 1977.
Crevalcore. 1906. Milan, Lombardi, 1991.
Duello d'anime. 1911. *Neera*, edited by Benedetto Croce, Milan, Garzanti, 1942, pp. 501–654.
Il castigo. 1881. Turin, L. Roux, 1891.
Il marito dell'amica. 1885. Milan, Galli, 1891.
Il romanzo della fortuna. 1905. Milan Antongini, 1906.

L'amuleto. 1897. *Neera*, edited by Benedetto Croce, Milan, Garzanti, 1942, pp. 419–500.
L'indomani. 1890. Palermo, Sellerio, 1990.
La Regaldina. 1883. Milan, Dumolard, 1884.
La vecchia casa. 1900. Milan, Treves, 1910.
Lydia. 1887. Neera, edited by Benedetto Croce, Milano, Garzanti, 1942, pp. 177–320.
Nel sogno. 1893. Sesto S. Giovanni, Madella, 1917.
Rogo d'amore. 1914. Milan, Treves, 1914.
Senio. 1892. Milan, Baldini & Castoldi, 1900.
Teresa. 1886. Edited by Luigi Badacci, Turin, Einaudi, 1976.
Un nido. 1880. Lecco, Periplo, 1994.
Un romanzo. 1876. Milan, G. Brigola, 1877.
Una passione. 1902. Milan, Sandron, 1903.
Vecchie catene. 1878. Milan, Treves, 1920.

Autobiographies

Confessioni letterarie. 1891. *Neera*, edited by Benedetto Croce, Milano, Garzanti, 1942, pp. 871–809.
Una giovinezza del secolo XIX. 1919. Milan, Cogliati, 1919.

Short Story Collections

Conchiglie. 1905. Rome, Voghera, 1905.
Fiori. 1921. Florence, Salani, 1921.
Iride. 1881. Milan, Baldini & Castoldi, 1905.
La freccia del parto. 1883. Milan, Baldini & Castoldi, 1901.
La sottana del diavolo. 1912. Milan, Garzanti, 1944.
La villa incantata. 1900. Livorno, Belforte, 1901.
Novelle gaie. 1879. Milan, G. Brigola, [18…].
Voci della notte. 1893. Naples, Luigi Pierro, 1893.

Essay Volumes

Battaglie per un'idea. 1898. Milan, Baldini & Castoldi, 1898.
Dizionario d'igiene per le famiglie (with Paolo Mantegazza). 1881. Edited by Maria Corti, Milano, Scheiwiller, 1985.
Fotografie matrimoniali. 1885. Catania, Giannotta, 1900.
Il libro di mio figlio. 1891. *Neera*, edited by Benedetto Croce, Milano, Garzanti, 1942, pp. 701–749.
Il secolo galante. 1900. Florence, Barbèra, 1900.
L'amor platonico. 1896. *Neera*, edited by Benedetto Croce, Milano, Garzanti, 1942, pp. 751–775.
La coscienza del fanciullo. 1908. Rome, Nuova Antologia, 1908.

Le idee di una donna. 1903. *Neera*, edited by Benedetto Croce, Milano, Garzanti, 1942, pp. 777–867.
Profili, impressioni, e ricordi di viaggi. 1919. Milan, L.F. Cogliati, 1920.
Un idealista. Alberto Sormani. 1898. Milan, Galli & Raimondi, 1898.

Poetry

Il canzoniere della nonna. 1908. Milan, L.F. Cogliati, 1908.
Poesie. 1919. Milan, L.F. Cogliati, 1919.

Theater

Maura. 1886. Comedy performed at Teatro Manzoni in Milan by Compagnia Torelli.

Notes

1 August Comte (1798–857) was a French philosopher known as the founder of sociology and positivism. His works include the six-volume publication of his philosophy titled *Cours de philosophie positive* (1830–42).
2 Cesare Lombroso (1835–909) was an Italian criminologist whose views on criminals brought about a shift in criminology, now discredited, that was focused on the scientific study of criminals in works such as *L'uomo delinquente* (1876) and La donna delinquente, la prostituta e la donna normale (1893).
3 Paul Julius August Moebius (1853–907) was a German neurologist whose production includes works on the topic of female inferiority such as *L'inferiorità mentale della donna* (1900).
4 Theories on women's physical and mental weakness, presented in the works of Darwinist and positivist thinkers such as Auguste Comte, Charles Darwin and Cesare Lombroso, thrived within late nineteenth-century European positivist culture. Female physical and intellectual inferiority were promoted as a logical consequence of the natural selection worldview, which posited the male species as exposed to far greater selective pressures and therefore more evolved physically and intellectually than the female species.
5 It seems that women, gifted at developing a seed of life within themselves for nine months, to give birth to it amongst the pains of labor, to raise it with an intelligent patience that verges on extraordinary, are usually incapable of regular poetic gestations: their artistic deliveries are almost always premature: rather, the birth immediately follows conception, and the newborn is then thrown out on the street, lacking every assistance that it would require. Croce, La letteratura della nuova Italia, vol. 2, p. 362. All translations of primary and secondary sources are mine.
6 Anna Maria Mozzoni (1837–920) is commonly regarded as the founder of the women's movement in Italy. Her work *La donna e i suoi rapporti*

sociali (1864), a feminist critique of Italian family law, was written on the occasion of the revision to the Italian Civil Code after the country's unification in 1861. Anna Kuliscioff (1857–925) was a Russian-born feminist and socialist active mainly in Italy, where she studied and practiced medicine and was one of the first women in Italy to graduate from university in medicine.

7 Neera, Matilde Serao, Grazia Deledda, Marchesa Colombi, Bruno Sperani, Carolina Invernizio, Contessa Lara, Regina di Luanto, Emma, Annie Vivanti, Luigia Codemo, Caterina Percoto, Regina di Luanto, Maria Messina and Anna Franchi were the principal women writers active in Italy in the last quarter of the nineteenth century.

8 A complete chronological list of Neera's works (by genre) is included at the end of this chapter.

9 The critical appraisal of Teresa was unanimous and widespread. See Zambon, "La narrativa realista nei romanzi d'autrice di fine Ottocento" 175, for an overview of the critical attention *Teresa* received.

10 In a letter to Angiolo Orvieto in 1898, Neera listed the translations of her novels up to that point. See Arslan and Zambon 212.

11 See Arlan "La galassia salvata. Scrivere per mestiere, scrivere per vocazione."

12 A notable exception are the *L'amica geniale* (2011) series of novels by Elena Ferrante which have become international bestsellers and the subject for an HBO series.

13 I would like to acknowledge the contribution to this issue of research conducted together with my colleague Sharon Hecker on the topic of women's intellectual and cultural labor.

14 See *Arslan, Dame, galline e regine.* 69 and 140. For criticism regarding the two faces of Neera, see Merry 286–291, Nozzoli 1–40, Pacifici 56, Wood 26–39.

15 See Libreria delle Donne di Milano 145–177, Diotima 9–79 and Muraro 3–35.

16 Neera confirmed the continuity in 1903 in a letter to Benedetto Croce: "ognuno di essi [romanzi] risponderebbe ad un concetto etico che sta in fondo a quasi tutti i miei romanzi." See Arslan and Folli 50.

17 As will be discussed further in Chapter 3 of this volume, Capuana dedicated the second edition of *Homo* and the third edition of *Giacinta* to Neera, respectively, in 1888 and 1889. Neera responded by dedicating her Confessioni *letterarie* to Capuana in 1891. Capuana and Neera maintained an intense epistolary exchange between 1881 and 1885. See Arslan, "Luigi Capuana e Neera: Corrispondenza inedita 1881–85."

18 In addition to *Una giovinezza del secolo XIX*, the collection of essays *Profili, impressioni, e ricordi di viaggi* and the volume *Poesie* were also published posthumously in 1919.

19 For a detailed study of woman's legal status in late nineteenth- and early twentieth-century Italy, see Galoppini. For an overview of woman's rights in the European context, see Duby and Perot 51–88.

20 For a detailed study of Mozzoni's role in the Italian women's emancipation movement, see Pieroni Bortolotti and Odorisio and Turi 17–66.

21 For a detailed study of women's journals and their directors in fin-de-siècle Italy, see Buttafuoco 21–52.

22 They put in their work of art an element of their own, femininity; but nothing more… I am convinced that in the future, in the distant future, women will be what men are now; but then men will be other; and the distance will remain the same as that of today. Then men will leave to women the business of writing novels, lyrics, tragedies, comedies and, if they have gotten a taste for it, poetry; but they – I add – will not create anything new, because there will be nothing else to create in the forms of art. It will be an eternal repetition, until they get tired; which is a bit unlikely: women are stubborn.

23 When a literary content is impoverished and worn out, women, who always perceive historical movements late, master them, extracting it fresh and alive from the past; they rediscover it when their brothers have already buried it, and they arrange in a bombastic epilogue the elements that are about to disperse.

24 In their autobiographies, Neera, Ada Negri, Grazia Deledda and Sibilla Aleramo discuss their lack of formal education. See Zambon, "Leggere per scrivere" 287–324.

25 See Kroha 1–6, Nozzoli 1 – 40, Morandini 5–24, Rasy 7–36. Other studies include Frabotta, Costa-Zalessow, Cutrufelli, Petrignani, Lazzaro-Weis and Marrotti. In the same period, studies in the Anglo-American context also focused on recognizing a female literary tradition. See Showalter 3–36.

26 Italian women's culture must be brought out of the idea of exception and rare anomaly, and it must move towards a healthy complementarity of vision and discussion, linking male and female texts so that they interact with each other, so that mutual influences can be studied.

27 The date provided after each title refers to the text's first publication, whether in volume or in journal. The works are listed chronologically by year of publication and by genre.

References

Arslan, Antonia. *Dame, galline e regine. La scrittura femminile italiana fra '800 e '900*, edited by Marina Pasqui, Milan, Guerini, 1998.

———. "La galassia salvata. Scrivere per mestiere, scrivere per vocazione." *La galassia sommersa. Suggestioni sulla scrittura femminile italiana*, edited by Antonia Arslan and Saveria Chemotti, Venice, Il Poligrafo, 2008, pp. 11–13.

———."Luigi Capuana e Neera: Corrispondenza inedita 1881–1885." *Miscellanea di studi in onore di Vittore Branca*, edited by Antonia Arslan. Florence, Olschki, 1983, pp. 161–185.

——— and Anna Folli, editors. *Il concetto che ne informa. Benedetto Croce e Neera. Corrispondenza (1903–1917).* Naples, Edizioni Scientifiche Italiane, 1988.

——— and Patrizia Zambon, editors. *Il sogno aristocratico. Angiolo Orvieto e Neera. Corrispondenza 1889–1917.* Milan, Guerini, 1990.

Borgese, Giuseppe Antonio. *La vita e il libro. Seconda Serie.* Turin, Bocca, 1911.

———. *La vita e il libro. Terza Serie*. Bologna, Zanichelli, 1928.

Buttafuoco, Annarita. *Cronache femminili. Temi e momenti della stampa emancipazionista in Italia dall'Unità al Fascismo*. Siena, Dipartimento di Studi Storico-Sociali e Filosofici Università degli Studi di Siena, 1988.

Capuana, Luigi. *Letteratura femminile*, edited by Giovanna Finocchiaro Chimirri, Catania, CUECM, 1988.

Costa-Zalessow, Natalia, editor. *Scrittrici italiane dal XIII al XX secolo*. Ravenna, Longo, 1982.

Croce, Benedetto. *La letteratura della nuova Italia*. Bari, Laterza, 1948.

———, editor. *Neera*. Milan, Garzanti, 1942.

Cuda, Rosa. "Re-appropriation for a New Symbolic Order: The Search for Identity in the Poetry of Armanda Guiducci, Maria Luisa Spaziani and Olivia Gualteri Bernardi." *Writing and Performing Female Identity in Italian Culture*, edited by Virginia Picchietti and Laura A. Salsini, London, Palgrave Macmillan, 2017, pp. 43–57.

Cutrufelli, Maria Rosa. *Scritture, scrittrici*. Rome, Longanesi, 1988.

Dijkstra, Bram. *Idols of Perversity: Fantasies of Feminine Evil in Fin-de-Siècle Culture*. New York: Oxford UP, 1988.

Diotima. *Il pensiero della differenza sessuale*. Milan, Tartaruga, 1987.

Duby, Georges and Michelle Perrot. *Storia delle donne in Occidente. L'Ottocento*, edited by Geneviève Fraisse and Michelle Perrot, Roma-Bari, Laterza, 1991.

Ferruggia, Gemma et al. *La donna italiana descritta da scrittrici italiane in una serie di conferenze tenute all'Esposizione Beatrice di Firenze*. Florence, Civelli, 1890.

Frabotta, Biancamaria. *Letteratura al femminile*. Bari, De Donato, 1980.

Frau, Ombretta and Cristina Gragnani. "Nineteenth-Century Women Writers between Marginality and (Aspirations of) Inclusion: A Puzzling Balance." *Italian Women Writers, 1800–2000. Boundaries, Borders and Transgression*, edited by Patrizia Sambuco, Madison, Fairleigh Dickinson UP, 2015.

Galoppini, Anna Maria. *Il lungo viaggio verso la parità: diritti civili e politici delle donne dall'Unità ad oggi*. Bologna, Zanichelli, 1980.

Gilbert, Sandra and Susan Gubar. *The Madwoman in the Attic: The Woman Writer and the Nineteenth Century Literary Imagination*. New Haven, Yale UP, 1979.

Graziani, Carlo Alberto and Ines Corti. *I diritti delle donne*. Milan, Giuffrè, 1996.

Hallamore Caesar, Ann, Gabriella Romani and Jennifer Burns, editors. *The Printed Media in Fin-de-Siècle Italy. Publishers, Writers and Readers*. London, Legenda, 2011.

Kroha, Lucienne. *The Woman Writer in Late 19th Century Italy: Gender and the Formation of Literary Identity*. Lewiston, Mellen, 1992.

Lazzaro-Weis, Carol. *From Margins to Mainstream: Feminism and Fictional Modes in Italian Women's Writing, 1968–1990*. Philadelphia, U of Pennsylvania P, 1993.

Libreria delle Donne di Milano. *Non credere di avere dei diritti.* Turin, Rosenberg & Sellier, 1987.

Lombroso, Cesare and G. Ferrero. *La donna delinquente, la prostituta e la donna normale.* 1893. Turin, Bocca, 1915.

Marrotti, Maria Ornella. *Italian Women Writers from the Renaissance to the Present.* Pennsylvania, Pennsylvania State UP, 1991.

Merry, Bruce. "Neera." *Italian Women Writers. A Bio-Bibliographical Sourcebook*, edited by Rinaldina Russell, London, Greenwood, 1994, pp. 286–294.

Mitchell, Katharine. *Italian Women Writers: Gender and Everyday Life in Fiction and Journalism, 1870–1910.* Toronto, U of Toronto P, 2014.

——— and Helena Sanson, editors. *Women and Gender in Post-Unification Italy. Between Private and Public Spheres.* Oxford, Peter Lang, 2013.

Momigliano, Anna. "'The Ferrante Effect': In Italy Women Writers are Ascendant." *The New York Times*, 9 December 2019, https://www.nytimes.com/2019/12/09/books/elena-ferrante-italy-women-writers.html. Accessed 25 March, 2020.

Morandini, Giuliana. *La voce che è in lei. Antologia della narrativa femminile italiana tra '800 e '900.* Milan, Bompiani, 1980.

Muraro, Luisa. *L'ordine simbolico della madre.* Rome, Riuniti, 1991.

Neera. *Battaglie per un'idea.* 1898. Milan, Baldini & Castoldi, 1898.

Nozzoli, Anna. "Le letteratura femminile in Italia tra Ottocento e Novecento." *Tabù e coscienza. La condizione femminile nella letteratura italiana del Novecento.* Florence, Nuova Italia, 1978, pp. 1–40.

Odorisio, Maria Linda and Monica Turi. *Donna o cosa? I movimenti femminili in Italia dal Risorgimento a oggi.* Turin, Milvia Carrà, 1991.

Pacifici, Sergio. *The Modern Italian Novel from Capuana to Tozzi.* Carbondale, Southern Illinois UP, 1973.

Petrignani, Sandra. *Le signore della scrittura.* Milan, Tartaruga, 1983.

Picchietti, Virginia and Laura A. Salsini, editors. "Introduction." *Writing and Performing Female Identity in Italian Culture.* Cham, Palgrave Macmillan, 2017, pp. 1–15.

Pieroni Bortolotti, Franca. *Alle origini del movimento femminile in Italia. 1848–1892.* Turin, Einaudi, 1963.

Rasy, Elisabetta. *Le donne e la letteratura.* Rome, Riuniti, 1984.

Russell, Rinaldina, editor. *The Feminist Encyclopedia of Italian Literature.* Westport, Greenwood, 1997.

Sanguineti, Edoardo. "Madre due volte." *Giornalino secondo 1976–1977.* Turin, Einaudi, 1979, pp. 293–295.

Showalter, Elaine. *A Literature of Their Own: British Women Novelists from Bronte to Lessing.* Princeton, Princeton UP, 1977.

West, Rebecca. "Women in Italian." *Italian Studies in North America*, edited by Massimo Ciavolella and Amilcare A. Iannucci, Ottawa, Dovehouse, 1994, pp. 195–212.

Wood, Sharon. *Italian Women's Writing 1860–1994*. London, Athlone, 1995.

Zambon, Patrizia. "La narrativa realista nei romanzi d'autrice di fine Ottocento." *Problemi*, vol. 108, 1997, pp. 166–177.

———. "Leggere per scrivere. La Formazione autodidattica delle scrittrici tra Otto e Novecento: Neera, Ada Negri, Grazia Deledda, Sibilla Aleramo." *Studi Novecenteschi*, vol. 16, no. 38, 1989, pp. 287–324.

1 Growing up Female in Fin-de-Siècle Italy

Anna Radius Zuccari was born in Milan on May 7, 1846, into a middle-class family. She lived the first 20 years of her life in the family's home in the center of Milan, in Corso Vittorio Emanuele, with periods spent during the summers at her mother's family home in Caravaggio and her father's family home in Casalmaggiore, both small towns not far from Milan. As Neera recounts in her autobiography *Una giovinezza del secolo XIX*, written in the last year of her life as she was confined to her bed due to illness, her childhood was marked by the premature death of her mother Maddalena Manusardi when she was ten: "La morte di mia madre volta una pagina della mia vita. Chiude un periodo della mia umile storia e la figura più angusta di tutte doveva restare nel mio cervello immaturo come una forma evanescente, una pallida donna, della quale non ricordo né lo sguardo, né la voce" [My mother's death turned a page in my life. It closes a period of my humble history and the darkest figure of all had to remain in my immature brain like an evanescent form, a pale woman, whose eyes and voice I cannot remember] (65). It is interesting to note, as will be discussed further later, that although Neera exalts maternity and the maternal instinct in her narrative and theoretical production, her personal maternal point of reference remained at best a vague memory. Neera's father, on the other hand, would be an influential figure in her life, one she immensely respected. In her autobiographical writings Neera dedicates several pages to describing her father Fermo Zuccari, a respected architect who held the positions of municipal councilor and honorary member of the Accademia di Brera, and the influence he exerted on the development of her personality and her desire to become a writer. In the emotionally deprived environment in which Neera lived after the death of her mother, a special role was reserved for the paternal figure. In her autobiographical writings, she refers to herself as the continuer of her father's morality and ideals, recounting how she found strength in following his example after his death in 1866, an event that constituted another traumatic event in her life:

> La vita ci aveva divisi, la morte ci univa in uno sposalizio d'anime. Nessuno ci avrebbe disgiunto mai più. Da quella notte il mio dolore divenne la mia forza. Incominciai allora veramente a vivere con mio padre, a interrogarlo e in ogni circostanza difficile a pensare in qual modo si sarebbe comportato lui stesso. Tenendolo così sempre presente mi sembrava di prolungare il suo soggiorno sulla terra e, poiché era entrato a far parte della mia vita interiore, non avevo quasi bisogno di parlargli: lo sentivo respirare nel respiro della mia coscienza. ... (*Una giovinezza* 227)[1]

Neera's attachment to her father, sublimated in death, constitutes the profound identification with this figure who represents a source of strength and inspiration for her, as portrayed in her autobiographical writings, and who serves as a model for the representation of the paternal figure in many of her novels. As will be discussed further ahead, Neera's representation of familial relations in several of her novels reveals an autobiographical origin. In novels such as *Addio!* (Farewell!, 1877), *Il marito dell'amica* (The friend's husband, 1884) and *La vecchia casa* (The old house, 1900), it is possible to observe the conceptual and lexical parallels with the portrayal of the father-daughter relationship in Neera's autobiographical writings. In *Confessioni letterarie*, she writes regarding her father that she learned from him to despise all that was vile, low and ignoble (883). In a similar fashion, for example, *Addio!*'s protagonist Valeria admits the profound influence her father's example and teachings had on the formation of her moral standards, based on scorn for cowardliness and hypocrisy and regard for honesty. (Neera, *Addio!* 13). In both Neera's life and her fiction, the paternal figure serves as a role model for the daughter, while the maternal figure is either absent or inadequate. The father nurtures the daughter's intellect, often in the absence of a son/brother, while the mother is not in a position to do so, often due to illness or death. The daughter must become a woman, but she finds herself unprepared for the role she is expected to fill. However, it is important to note, as will be discussed in more detail later, that at times in Neera's narrative production, the paternal exerts a negative and oppressive influence upon the daughter figure. Examination of the complex familial relationships in Neera's literary production allows a better understanding of the development of her female protagonists but also of the socio-historical realm they portray, the one inhabited also by Neera, a realm characterized by female subordination within social and familial spheres. The similarities between the autobiographical and narrative portrayals of the familial relationship point to a personal source for Neera's representation of the daughter's desire to conform to the paternal model.

Neera's portrayal of her mother and father, and the influence they exerted on her development recall the familial relationships represented in the autobiographical text of another woman writer of the period, Sibilla Aleramo's *Una donna* (A woman, 1906):

> L'amore per mio padre mi dominava unico. Alla mamma volevo bene, ma per il babbo avevo un'adorazione illimitata; e di questa differenza mi rendevo conto, senza osar cercarne le cause. Era lui il luminoso esemplare per la mia piccola individualità, lui che mi rappresentava la bellezza della vita: un istinto mi faceva ritenere provvidenziale il suo fascino. Nessuno gli somigliava: egli sapeva tutto e aveva sempre ragione. (Aleramo 1–2)[2]

It is interesting to note that it is the father figure, rather than the mother, who serves as a source of intellectual and moral inspiration in the autobiographical writings of these two important fin-de-siècle women writers, both of whom promote examples of female autonomy in their works. In *Speculum of the Other Woman* (1974), Luce Irigaray explains the absence of the maternal figure as linked to the devaluing within Western patriarchal culture of the mother as a role model for the daughter (39–40). It is important to note, as will be discussed later, that Neera comes to oppose the devaluation of the mother within society through the reappropriation in her theoretical and later narrative production of the maternal figure as a positive figure and the maternal instinct and role as a source of empowerment for women.

Neera's autobiographical writings reveal how the truly dark period in her upbringing began after the death of her mother, which was followed a few years later by the end of her schooling at age 14. From that point onward, Neera's daily existence was governed by two elderly aunts, whose severity and lack of affection profoundly influenced the development of the writer's already melancholically inclined nature:

> Incominciò allora la mia esistenza casalinga, metodica come una regola di convento; alzata alle otto, rifatta la camera e la sala di ricevimento (dove non entrava mai nessuno) preso posto verso le dieci al tavolino da lavoro, dal quale non mi movevo più sino alle quattro, con una zia da una parte e una zia dall'altra; alle quattro preparavo la tavola, alle quattro e mezzo si pranzava; alla sera lavoro di nuovo, generalmente calze, una zia da una parte una zia dall'altra, sino all'ora di andare a letto. (Neera, *Una giovinezza* 90–91)[3]

Entrusted to the watchful eyes of her aunts, Neera's days revolved around the monotonous duty which came to dominate her time: sewing and mending socks. It is evident from the above description that Neera's years as a young woman within the domestic confines still weighed upon her later years as she wrote her autobiography. Those years remained within her memory as time wasted, as an inflicted injustice and as a deception made perhaps more painful by the fact that it was enforced by other women, themselves victims, who became oppressors themselves in a painful cycle.

In 1871, at the age of 25, Neera married Milanese banker Emilio Radius, finally escaping the oppressive atmosphere of her years spent with her elderly aunts. They had two children, Adolfo, who became an engineer, and Maria, who married journalist and editor Guido Martinelli. Rather quickly, Neera began to make a name for herself in Milanese literary circles, frequenting literary salons, entering into contact with leading intellectual figures and publishing in 1876 her first novel, *Un romanzo,* in installments in the literary journal *Pungolo.* During her career she became one of the most recognized female literary voices in Italy, publishing articles, short stories and novels on the pages of the most prestigious journals of the day.

Neera remained throughout her life firmly anchored to her home in Milan. In *Ricordando Neera* (Remembering Neera), written the year after Neera's death, Serao describes a visit to the writer's home in the center of Milan in Via Borgospesso, reflecting on how the profoundly middle-class Milanese essence of Neera's home both intimately reflects and contrasts with her personality:

> Già le penombre crepuscolari entravano nel modesto salottino, ove stavamo; e confondevano linee e colori di quell'ambiente, schiettamente borghese e lombardo, di cui *Neera* nulla aveva mutato, per un pietoso rispetto del passato, per una lunga

> consuetudine di vita, che le era piaciuto di continuare, anche se in perfetto contrasto con la ricchezza e la originalità della sua ardente fantasia. (22)[4]

Serao reflects upon the conflicting facets of Neera's identity, her reserved and private life as bourgeois wife and mother as opposed to her "other" life as a nationally and internationally successful writer, perhaps because she also, as wife, mother and writer, felt the weight of these conflicting roles for women writers of the time.

Writing Personal Experiences and Vocation

Neera manages to "escape" from the context of emotional deprivation and limitations of life with her aunts, which she compares to the seclusion of life in a cloistered convent, by finding refuge and consolation in her daydreams and by creating through reading and writing a separate, parallel world inhabited by ideas, inspirations, hopes and desires. In "Neera (1846–1918). The World Seen from the Window: Reading, Writing, and the Power of Fantasy" (2013), Olivia Santovetti notes that "Neera's passion for reading and her determination to becoming a writer emerge as a vital strategy-of which she will become increasingly aware-to cope with and overcome the limitation and segregation experienced growing up in the Italian patriarchal society" (388). The restricted atmosphere of those years heightens Neera's sensibility,[5] which she describes as above average, and leads her to transcribe on the page the experiences she is unable to live out in person:

> Continuavo a scrivere, perché erano questi i momenti più belli della mia giornata, una valvola per mezzo della quale sfogavo pensieri, desideri, rimpianti; … I piaceri della fantasia hanno sui piaceri del senso questo grande vantaggio di non trovare ostacoli alla libera espansione; la fantasia non conosce limiti né leggi; (Neera, *Una giovinezza* 210–211)[6]

Writing and an irresistible vocation account for how Neera overcomes the isolation of those years to pursue becoming a *scrittrice* [woman writer], as she further reveals in the following passage from her *Confessioni letterarie*[7]:

> Tutto, intorno a me, era contrario alla mia passione. L'educazione incompleta, l'ambiente ristretto, la mancanza d'affettuosità,

> la quasi nessuna comunicazione col mondo, e niente emulazione, niente stimolo, niente aiuto – nemmeno quella ostilità che alcune volte è sferza e sprone. (885)[8]

Neera finds no support or stimulation of any kind in this environment, but only indifference, which she describes as even harder to overcome than an obstacle. In *Una giovinezza del secolo XIX*, Neera contrasts her childhood environment and influences with those described by fellow woman writer Matilde Serao, who writes of satisfying her hunger for knowledge as a young woman through daily contact with intellectuals. Unlike Serao, whose father was a journalist and who grew up within the thriving Neapolitan literary and journalistic circles, Neera had no contact with intellectual circles in her youth. In *Confessioni letterarie*, she reveals the conflict between her artistic inclinations and the limitations of her surroundings and how her avid search for reading material of any kind, from the books in her father's library to the printed paper used by shopkeepers to package goods, serves as a way of compensating for her lack of exposure to the outside world (Neera, *Confessioni* 875). Furthermore, her portrayal of her years in school reveals the limited nature of a scholastic training that also failed to constitute an incentive to learning. In *Una giovinezza del secolo XIX*, Neera recalls her dislike of school and sense of relief when her studies ended at age 14, justifying such emotions with a description of the unorganized nature of the education she received:

> Il difetto principale di quelle lezioni era la mancanza assoluta di un concetto regolatore. Invece di incominciare dal principio e procedere gradualmente con nozioni chiare, legate da un nesso logico di continuità, a fanciulle ignoranti, quali noi eravamo, ci scaraventavano addosso una specie di estratto Liebig indigesto e confuso sull'origine delle lingue romanze. Un altro giorno erano idee generali sul secolo XV. (26)[9]

Neera's memory of those years of study, depicted as lacking direction and logical connections between the topics studied, provides insight into the nature of education for young women at that time. Although both girls and boys were required by law to attend elementary school as of 1859, schools were separated according to gender, and this division allowed for the existence of a separate but not equal condition between schools for boys and those for girls. Acknowledging her lack of a formal education, Neera candidly reveals the preparatory studies she undertook before writing her novels: "calze, camicie e calze" [stockings, shirts and stockings] (*Una giovinezza* 160). Although she was not stimulated by her surroundings at home or by her studies at school, books and the act of writing represented a source of fascination for her already at a young age (Neera, *Una giovinezza* 157).

Regardless of the restrictive familial and social atmosphere that surrounded her formative years, Neera persevered in her literary vocation, writing her first novel at the age of 16, a romance novel in which "l'amore felice, coronato dal matrimonio, doveva far dimenticare le pene incredibili sopportate dall'eroina" [happy love, crowned by marriage, was meant to help forget the incredible suffering endured by the heroine] (Neera, *Confessioni* 890). Although Neera destroyed her early literary creations, she later recognized the embryonic elements of her future literary style in those works:

> Osservavo fin da allora la vita, ma quelle osservazioni inconscie ed oggettive andavano a formare i diversi strati dei lavori futuri, a mettere i germi e le radici dell'analisi naturalistica, che doveva svilupparsi più tardi, senza partito preso, così come mi accadde di fare ogni cosa, sempre, per evoluzione spontanea. (*Confessioni* 891)[10]

Character analysis, emotional involvement and psychological introspection characterize Neera's writing and her portrayal of the female reality, revealing her ability to investigate with extreme insight even the most hidden aspects of the female psychology. Neera instills in her protagonists her own personal experiences and observations of suffering while also providing a clear analysis of the female situation at every social level. With regard to her novel *Teresa*, for example, Neera reveals the following autobiographical source for the protagonist's plight novel in *Una giovinezza*:

> Non altrimenti la patetica storia della donna a cui manca l'amore germinava da lunghi anni nel segreto delle mie sofferenze, nelle ingiustizie di cui ero stata vittima, nella persecuzione che aveva attossicato fin dalle sorgenti la mia ingenua giovinezza. Era il dramma di tante anime femminili che si era ripercosso attraverso la deviazione di un'anima sulla speciale sensibilità dell'anima mia. (213–214)[11]

Neera's heightened sensibility, together with her own personal experiences of suffering, provides the foundation for the representation of female oppression in her narrative production. She compensates for the lacuna in her literary training and her limited contact with intellectual circles through a refined sensibility and experiences of another kind. In *Italian Women Writers: Gender and Everyday Life in Fiction and Journalism* (2014), Katharine Mitchell notes regarding domestic fiction by women authors that "[t]he female narrator tells the story of 'real' women from *her* point of view: as if to recover hundreds of years of a majority of silent female voices, an all-female world is being depicted in the texts" (26). Neera's personal experiences as a young woman growing up in late nineteenth-century Italy lend not only a special insight but also a new kind of narratorial authority to her narrative portrayals of the female condition. Mirroring the writer's own origins and social status, Neera's novels for the most part feature protagonists from middle-class settings, although, as will be discussed further ahead, some novels dedicate attention to the female condition in lower- and upper-class contexts as well. In her 1992 article "C'è un fantasma sotto lo scialle" (There is a ghost under the shawl), Maria Corti notes that Neera's production presents "uno studio sottile e lucido delle insoddisfazioni femminili in ogni strato sociale" [a subtle and lucid study of female dissatisfactions at every social level] (26).

Neera is not the only woman writer of her time to deny the importance of a scholastic formation in favor of sensibility and personal experiences, especially those deriving from emotional and environmental privations and adversity. In the article "Leggere per scrivere" (Reading for writing, 1989), Patrizia Zambon notes a similarity between Neera and fellow fin-de-siècle women writers Ada Negri, Grazia Deledda and Sibilla Aleramo in the privileging of an uncommon sensibility that outweighs academic studies. Zambon observes that all four writers are "convinte che la capacità di scrittura sia eminentemente sensibilità interiore – che oltretutto si affina, si approfondisce nelle esperienze di solitudine e nelle esperienze di sofferenze – e capacità di osservazione e di analisi, anch'esse strettamente legate alla solitudine" [convinced that the ability to write was eminently inner sensitivity - refined, deepened in experiences of loneliness and suffering - and the ability to observe and analyze, also closely related to loneliness] (301–302). As discussed earlier, contemporary male critics noted stylistic and linguistic imperfections as characteristic of female literary production, often as a way of affirming the inferior quality of women writers' work. In "'The Ferrante Effect': In Italy Women Writers are Ascendant" (2019) Anna Momigliano refers to Italy as "a country where self-referential virtuosity is often valued over storytelling, emotional resonance and issues like sexism or gender roles," offering a possible explanation for why the style and subject matter privileged by many women writers failed to gain recognition. By claiming personal experiences of solitude and suffering as the source of inspiration and subject matter for their work, fin-de-siècle women writers affirmed a new kind of authority for the figure of writer while also proposing the worth of their production based on experiences other than scholastic training.

Women Writers and Pseudonyms: Between Private and Public Spheres

Although Neera was one of the most active and recognized women writers of her time, she led a very private personal life, about which not much is known beyond the years of her youth, intimately narrated in her autobiography *Una giovinezza del XIX secolo.* She wrote all of her works under the pseudonym Neera, chosen at a young age for its harmonious sound.[12] The writer links her use of a pseudonym to her need for privacy: "Non ho mai compreso la vanità letteraria, anzi il mio orrore della notorietà era così forte, che allorquando mi trovai al punto di scendere nell'arena presi uno pseudonimo, colla ferma convinzione di innalzare una barriera inaccessibile fra me e l'opera mia" [I never understood literary vanity, indeed my horror of notoriety was so strong, that when I found myself at the point of descending into the arena I took a pseudonym, with the firm conviction of raising an inaccessible barrier between me and my work] (*Confessioni* 890). In comparing the decision to begin her literary career to entering an arena, Neera underscores the reality of the literary profession as a battle for women, one they fight not only externally but also from within. The external nature of the women writers' struggle to assert themselves as writers can be understood from the following excerpt from *Le idee di una donna* in which Neera discusses the difficulties encountered in the male-dominated literary circles of the period:

> Ognuno di essi [scrittori maschili] era ben disposto a festeggiare la scrittrice quando nel suo interno la considerava come un leggiadro pupazzetto del suo medesimo sogno, inoffensivo, divertente, forse utile. Ma è tutt'altra cosa se la donna diviene una rivale nella concorrenza. … Al punto in cui la lotta si impegna seriamente, la differenza del sesso è cagione di

> astio maggiore. È allora che la scrittrice si sente straniera in mezzo a quegli uomini inaspriti che hanno gettato la maschera della galanteria, ripresi dalla atavica brutalità dell'animale in guerra. (832–833)[13]

Neera reveals the antagonism experienced by women writers in competition with their male counterparts for recognition and the strength of character needed to carry on and succeed. Her own sense of alienation as a woman writer perhaps influenced her to dedicate attention within her narrative and theoretical work to the theme of female alienation in society in its various manifestations, from spinsterhood and arranged marriages to female dissatisfaction within marriage.

The decision by many women writers of the period to use a pseudonym can also be linked to the conflict of roles that derived from the choice of a profession over the duties of wife and mother. Neera was not alone in her use of a *nom de plume*, as many Italian women writers of the period, such as Evelina Cattermole Mancini (Contessa Lara), Maria Antonietta Torriani (Marchesa Colombi) and Beatrice Speraz (Bruno Sperani), also published their work under an alias. In *The Woman Writer in Late 19th Century Italy: Gender and the Formation of Literary Identity* (1992), Lucienne Kroha attributes the widespread use of pen names by women writers in this period to the desire to protect their private identity as women from the public one of writer. Within this context, it is interesting to consider Luigi Capuana's 1880 review of Neera's novel *Un nido*, in which he reflects on how a pseudonym indicates the woman writer's dualistic existence and seclusion within the confines of the family and home:

> Il pseudonimo di una signora, soprattutto, significa: Badate! Io voglio essere due persone: una, la donna – fanciulla, madre di famiglia, zitellona, - che vive pei parenti e pegli amici, che non isdegna nessuno dei suoi doveri domestici, previdente, massaia, infermiera, ora allegra, ora coi nervi, spesso impensierita delle troppe cure del suo piccolo regno; l'altra, la scrittrice che mette fuori ogni anno dei volumi composti non si sa quando, nei momenti rubati al sonno e alle preoccupazioni della vita giornaliera. (*Studii sulla letteratura contemporanea* 86)[14]

In identifying the difficulty for late nineteenth-century women writers, unlike their male counterparts, in finding the time to dedicate themselves to an occupation other than those of wife and mother or obedient daughter, Capuana identifies the pressures on women to fulfill specific roles and duties within society. All women had one profession that preceded all others: the selfless woman who put the interests and needs of others before her own. Capuana describes the profession of writer as adaptable only to the male lifestyle, which leaves men free during the fruitful hours of the day to dedicate themselves to writing, as opposed to women's obligation to carry out their "day jobs" as mothers and wives. The separation of women from their identities as professional writers juxtaposes their creative ability to the reality of their lives within the family domain, as Capuana's comments further confirm:

> Le persone difficili, i critici che fanno mestiere di scandalizzarsi di tutto, quando s'incontrano in alcune pagine dell'*Addio* e delle *Vecchie catene* ove la passione parlava il suo caldo e irragionevole linguaggio, ne dedussero che l'autrice di quelle pagine doveva aver sentito qualcosa di quei colpevoli ardori. Invece esse erano il parto di una donnina savia, di una mamma affettuosa che, prima di sedersi al tavolino e intinger la penna, aveva messo amorosamente a letto i suoi bimbi, e avea dato gli ordini più minuti pel governo della sua modesta famiglia. (*Studii sulla letteratura contemporanea* 87)[15]

Capuana reveals the complexities of the profession of writer for women at that time, forced to divide their time between familial and professional duties but also facing speculation on their sources of inspiration for the events narrated in their works. How could a *signora*, expected to fulfill and uphold the roles of wife and mother, know enough to offer narration on such unacceptable topics as adulterous love and passion? In *Letters and Labyrinths: Women Writing/Cultural Codes* (1997), Diane Cousineau suggests that the use of a pseudonym puts into question the notion of the writer's unified self as well as the authenticity of the written text itself: "the signature attests to the existence of a responsible and unified self that assures the truth of the letter's body" (27). Through the use of a pseudonym, women writers freed themselves from the speculation that readers and critics alike likely drew regarding the written word and personal experience, protecting their privacy but also their ability to express themselves as they wished without fear of social retaliation. The use of a pseudonym provides an important example of the intricacies of the literary career for fin-de-siècle women writers: the issue was not merely being a woman – the challenges facing women writers depended also upon social class, education level and various aspects of identity that affected public perception of an individual.

Fin-de-Siècle Italian Women Writers and Their Literary Mothers, Daughters and Sisters

It is important to note that Neera and contemporary women writers, members of a first generation of Italian women writers, did not possess strong female literary models that could serve to legitimate them as writers and the style and content of their production as worthy. Zambon notes, in fact, that although the careers of women writers had become normalized by the end of the nineteenth century in much of Europe and America, in Italy, this was not the case: "In Italia in qualche modo vive ancora sul finir del secolo l'idea di una eccezionalità e quella di una particolarità della donna scrittrice" [In Italy somehow the idea of exceptionality regarding the woman writer continues to exist at the turn of the century] (293). It is important to consider, as discussed previously, that the model of writer at that time was based on exclusively male characteristics and lifestyles, a fact that undoubtedly created conflict for many women writers caught between constructing with their work a female literary tradition and facing society's negation of female literary models. For fin-de-siècle Italian women writers, the search for literary mothers meant looking beyond national borders. Kroha suggests George Eliot and Madame de Stael as literary models for Neera, analyzing the influence of de Stael's *Corinne ou l'Italie* (Corinne or Italy, 1807) and Eliot's *The Mill on the Floss* (1860) on *Teresa*: "A close comparative reading of *Teresa* and *The Mill on the Floss* reveals that Teresa is none other than a Maggie Tulliver of the Italian provinces" (Kroha 94). In the essay "La parte della donna" (The Woman's part), Neera acknowledges the typical, for the time, female upbringing of two leading women writers who nonetheless achieved literary success, suggesting again that formal scholastic training is not a prerequisite for succeeding within the literary profession:

> Le due grandi scrittrici del secolo, George Elliot and George Sand, passarono i primi trent'anni della loro vita, l'una a manipolar burro, l'altra a fabbricar conserve: forse nessuna, ripeto, delle fanciulle che ora si vogliono tirar su per scrittrici (povere fanciulle!) scriverà *Il mulino sulla Floss* o *Consuelo*. Ma

> anche è necessario persuadersi che migliaia di donne, le quali non scrissero romanzo alcuno, sono, o per intelligenza o per beneficio influsso delle loro anime o per ricca sensibilità, benemerite al pari o più della Eliot e della Sand. (Neera, *Le idee di una donna* 801)[16]

With the reference to "povere fanciulle!" (poor girls!), Neera alerts potential literary daughters to the difficulties of the profession, while proceeding, however, to recognize the potential for becoming writers that exists among women who lead ordinary lives. Affirmations such as the one above reflect the tension that exists between Neera's status as a revolutionary figure for the time, a woman defying traditional female roles, and the at times conflicting messages that emerge from her writing. Kroha suggests that Neera "represses and even denies her sense of solidarity with other women writers in order to avoid acknowledging the break with tradition represented by her writing and by *Teresa* in particular" (96). In place of an established sisterhood between women writers of the fin-de-siècle period, Mitchell suggests the term "sisterhood-in-the-making," given "the emphasis on the common themes in their domestic fiction and journalism, which offered first-hand 'social documentary' of predominantly middle-class female experience to their female readers, told from a woman's perspective" (110).

It is interesting to note that the privacy of the epistolary genre, as I discuss in Chapter 4 of this study, allows women writers the freedom to communicate a sense of solidarity amongst themselves, recognizing and encouraging their talent and literary achievements. Neera acknowledges in her theoretical writings the difficulty for women writers in expressing themselves publicly as opposed to privately. In *Le idee di una donna*, she writes, "A scrivere per sé ogni donna intelligente riesce a meraviglia. Scrivere per il pubblico è tutt'altra cosa ed è cosa difficilissima, che non si insegna e non si impara, ed anche quando la si sa è traditrice sirena che troppe volte trascina a naufragare fin sotto i fanali del porto" [Every intelligent woman can write for herself. Writing for the public is something quite different and it's a very difficult thing, that one can't teach or learn, and even when you know it, it's a traitorous siren that too many times drags you to sink under the lights of the port] (833). Neera's thoughts on a personal, intimate language utilized by women for themselves foreshadow modern feminist thought on female linguistic alienation. In the essay "Per una teoria della differenza sessuale" (For a theory of sexual difference, 1987), Adriana

Cavarero proposes a female order in the construction of a maternal language in opposition to the supposedly universal language of patriarchal society which forces women to express themselves with the "linguaggio dell'altro" [language of the other] (Cavarero 49). In her 1976 article "The Laugh of the Medusa," Hélène Cixous speaks of "*marked* writing," affirming that "writing has been run by a libidinal and cultural – hence political, typically masculine – economy," and that

> this is a locus where the repression of women has been perpetuated, ... where woman has never *her* turn to speak – this being all the more serious and unpardonable in that writing is precisely *the very possibility of change*, the space that can serve as a springboard for subversive thought, the precursory movement of a transformation of social and cultural structures. (879)

Neera addresses the issue of women writers' linguistic alienation in Italian literary circles of her time and points to the dangers for women in adopting a language that is often felt to be alien and traitorous. The ambivalent attitude displayed at times by Neera toward fellow and potential women writers and the profession itself offers another example of the complexities women writers faced as they operated between public and private spheres and struggled with bringing together the conflicting roles of woman and writer.

Neera's "Two Faces"

The episodes during Neera's career in which she emerged publicly as a detractor of the *questione femminile* have no doubt accounted through the years for categorizing her as conservative and antifeminist.[17] Bruce Merry notes, in fact, in the entry dedicated to Neera in *Italian Women Writers: A Bio-Bibliographical Sourcebook* (1994), that "main problem for her modern reader is the constant affirmation in her work of the values of motherhood and the duties or joys of the housewife" (286). Critics such as Sergio Pacifici reject an interpretation of Neera as essentially a feminist author, noting in *The Modern Italian Novel from Capuana to Tozzi* (1973) the "contradictions between the critical and the creative work" of her production (56). Unable to reconcile the "reazionario, classista, decisamente antifeminista" [reactionary, classist, decidedly antifeminist] aspect of Neera's theoretical writings with the intuitive feminism of her novels, Anna Nozzoli argues in *Tabù e coscienza* (Taboo and conscience, 1978) that Neera's ideas are "perigliosamente bilanciate tra tabù e coscienza, tra riconoscimento della dignità femminile e sua fruizione all'interno del nucleo familiare, tra realtà e mito" [perilously balanced between taboo and conscience, between recognition of female dignity and its use within the family, between reality and myth] (29).

There has been significant interest, however, in recent decades in the feminist aspect of Neera's narrative production, especially the novels of her trilogy *Teresa*, *Lydia* and *L'indomani*, and in understanding the apparent contradictions between her narrative and theoretical production.[18] In the 1976 reprint of *Teresa,* largely responsible for proposing Neera to the modern reader as a feminist author, Luigi Baldacci presents the novel as an essential document of the feminist spirit (vii). Although he lends special attention to *Teresa* as one of the best Italian novels of the last twenty years of the nineteenth century (v), Baldacci proposes the feminist aspect of all of Neera's narrative "nella misura in cui la donna è sentita come classe (oppressa) e non come ideale complemento dell'uomo" [to the extent that woman is felt as a class (oppressed) and not as an ideal complement of man] (vii). Baldacci rejects the notion of Neera as "complice del sistema" [accomplice of the system] (v), justifying contradictions observed in her production as the difference between representing reality, in the case of her novels, and theorizing an ideal, in the case of her essays. In the Introduction to the 1977 reprint of *Le idee di una donna* and *Confessioni letterarie*, Francesco Sanvitale interprets the feminist aspect of Neera's work in her refusal to aspire to the male model, a view shared also by Vittorio Spinazzola in his "Introduzione a Neera" (Intoduction to Neera) featured in *Ritratto di signora. Neera (Anna Radius Zuccari) e il suo tempo* (Portrait of a lady. Neera (Anna Radius Zuccari) and her time, 1999): "Quel che mi pare certo è che, se non femminista, Neera era energicamente antimaschilista. Dalle sue pagine traspare un risentimento forte contro il sesso dominante: i personaggi virili sono o egoisti brutali o fiacchi sognatori fallimentari" [What I think for sure is that, if not feminist, Neera was energetically anti-masculine. From her pages shines a strong resentment against the dominant sex: the virile characters are either brutal egoists or failed dreamers] (12).

Kroha views the apparent contradictions in Neera's production as deriving not only from the incompatibility of fiction and non-fiction, but from the conflicts that characterized her literary consciousness, torn between "being a professional and remaining a 'lady' in spite of it" (70). In *Italian Women's Writing 1860–1994* (1995), Sharon Wood attributes the "two faces" of Neera to the conflicting aspects of the time in which she lived: "The writing of Neera marks the drama of transition and adjustment which Italian society experienced in those years, torn between the old and the new" (27). In her 1998 essay "Ideologia e autorappresentazione" (Ideology and autorepresentation), Antonia Arslan notes that the dichotomy between theoretical and creative writing is not unique to Neera's case, stating:

> proprio le donne di successo – e 'di rispetto' – le punte di diamante dell'affermazione femminile in letteratura, si dimostrano … esitanti e incerte nel trarre in sede teorica le conseguenze di ordine emancipazionista e sociale che sembrerebbero logica conseguenza dei casi descritti nella loro narrativa. (168)[19]

For Neera, the act of writing is intimately related to the expression of her spirit, and she describes her literary style as characterized by spontaneity (*Confessioni* 891–892). She proudly claims her independence from blindly following literary schools or styles, acknowledging instead something unique as the inspiration for her literary production:

> Non apparterò mai a nessuna scuola, non seguirò mai nessun metodo, resterò sempre troppo realista per gli uni, troppo sentimentale per gli altri. Ma poiché tra gli uni e gli altri c'è pur qualcuno che mi accetta come sono, per quei pochi continuerò a scrivere – e meglio ancora che per quei pochi, per l'unico, divino che mi ispira - quello che, amico mio, non so chiamare diversamente di così: l'ideale nel reale. (*Confessioni* 34)[20]

She identifies the bringing together of two additional "separate spheres," the ideal and the real, as the two factors that best characterize her work and stimulate her to write, providing perhaps the best explanation to date for her "two faces" and offering today's reader a striking example for the time of a woman writer's fierce independence and recognition of her own self-worth.

Additional insight into Neera's "two faces" can be found in the various "separate spheres" she and other women writers of the period inhabited, not only those occupied by men versus women but also those occupied by male writers versus women writers, wives/

mothers versus professional writers, public versus private personas, emancipationists versus antifeminists, scholars versus the self-educated and many others. Such intersectionality characterizes Neera's experience as well as that of many women writers of her time, forced to navigate between various realms. Neera dwelled in all of these spheres, using her extraordinary sensibility and vocation to portray and bring attention to the issue that not only characterized her own personal existence but also that of her protagonists: the female reality in turn-of-the-century Italy.

Notes

1 Life had divided us, death united us in a marriage of souls. No one would ever separate us again. From that night on, my pain became my strength. Then I really began to live with my father, to question him and in all difficult circumstances to think how he would behave. Keeping him always in my mind in this way seemed to me to prolong his stay on earth and, since he had become part of my inner life, I hardly needed to talk to him: I could feel him breathing in the breath of my conscience.

2 The love for my father dominated me uniquely. I loved my mother, but I had unlimited adoration for my father, and I realized the difference, without daring to look for the causes. He was the shining example for my small individuality, he who represented the beauty of life to me: an instinct made me consider his charm providential. No one was like him: he knew everything and was always right.

3 Then began my homely existence, methodical as convent rule; up at eight o'clock, tidy the room and the living room (where no one ever went in) at about ten o'clock I was at the work table, from which I no longer moved until four o'clock, with an aunt on one side and an aunt on the other; at four o'clock I set the table, at half past four we ate; in the evening I worked again, usually on stockings, an aunt on one side and an aunt on the other, until bedtime.

4 Already the twilight shadows had entered the modest sitting room, where we were; and confused lines and colors of that typically bourgeois and Lombard environment, of which Neera had changed nothing, out of a merciful respect of the past, a lifelong habit which she enjoyed continuing, even if in perfect contrast with the richness and originality of her ardent imagination.

5 Several critics of Neera's work have commented on the influence of unhappy childhood circumstances on her literary style and production. See Croce, vol. 4, p. 128, Serao 6–8, Menasci 263–278, Corti 26 and Corda 55.

6 I kept on writing, because these were the most beautiful moments of my day, a valve through which I vented thoughts, desires, regrets; … The pleasures of fantasy have an enormous advantage over the pleasures of the senses, of not finding obstacles to free expansion; fantasy knows no limits or laws.

7 In *Confessioni letterarie,* Neera recalls her vocation for writing from a very young age, as in the following passages: "concludo colla persuasione di avere scritto sempre dal giorno in cui seppe tenere la penna" (873) and "ho nove anni, sono brutta, la mamma mi sgrida sempre, scrivo così" (873).

8 Everything around me was against my passion. The incomplete education, the restricted environment, the lack of affection, the almost no communication with the world, and no emulation, no stimulus, no help - not even that hostility that is sometimes lash and spur.

9 The main flaw in those lessons was the complete lack of a regulatory concept. Instead of starting from the beginning and gradually proceeding with clear notions, linked by a logical nexus of continuity, they provided us ignorant girls, as we were, with a kind of indigestible and confused beef extract about the origin of Romance languages. Another day there were general ideas about the 15th century.

10 I was observing life even then, but those unconscious and objective observations were forming the different layers of future work, creating the foundation for naturalistic analysis, which was to develop later, without calculation, as it happened to me to do everything, always, by spontaneous evolution.

11 Not otherwise, the pathetic story of the woman who lacks love had been germinating for many years in the secret of my sufferings, in the injustices of which I had been a victim, in the persecution that had disturbed my naive youth from the beginning. It was the drama of so many female souls that was reflected through the deviation of a soul on the special sensitivity of my soul.

12 Neera reveals the source of her pseudonym in the following passage from *Una giovinezza del secolo XIX*:

> Eccomi alla fine della mia vita di fanciulla, Neera non è ancor nata, quantunque il bellissimo nome scorto in un libro scolastico delle Odi di Orazio mi avesse già colpita in modo straordinario e così tenace che allorquando, più tardi, volli scegliere uno pseudonimo non tentai neppure di cercarne un altro. (216)

13 Each of them [male writers] was well-disposed to celebrate the writer when he saw her as a graceful puppet of his own dream, harmless, funny, perhaps useful. But it's quite different if the woman becomes a rival in the competition. ... At the point where the struggle is seriously engaged, the difference in sex is a major cause of resentment. It's then that the woman writer feels a stranger among those bitter men who have thrown down the mask of gallantry, taken up by the atavistic brutality of the animal at war.

14 A lady's pseudonym, above all, means: Beware! I want to be two people: one, the woman - maiden, mother of a family, spinster, - who lives for relatives and friends, who does not disdain any of her domestic duties, provident, housewife, nurse, now cheerful, now with nerves, often worrying about the too many cares of her little kingdom; the other, the writer who puts out every year some composed volumes, we do not know when, in the moments stolen from sleep and worries of daily life.

15 The difficult people, the critics who make a habit of scandalizing themselves about everything, when they meet in some pages of *Addio*! and *Le vecchie catene* where passion spoke its warm and unreasonable language, deduced that the author of those pages must have heard something of those guilty ardors. Instead they were the birth of a wise woman, a loving mother who, before sitting at the table and dipping her pen, had lovingly put her children to bed, and had given the most minute orders to the government of her modest family.

16 The two great women writers of the century, George Elliot and George Sand, spent the first thirty years of their lives, one manipulating butter, the other making preserves: perhaps none, I repeat, of the girls who now want to grow up to be writers (poor girls!) will write *The Mill on Floss* or *Consuelo*. But it is also necessary to persuade oneself that thousands of women, who did not write any novel, are, either for intelligence or for the benefit of their souls or for rich sensibility, as good as or more than Eliot and Sand.

17 Santovetti notes that

> the essays collected in the volume entitled *Le idee di una donna* (1903) are perfectly in line with the then partriarchal system of values according to which the place of the woman was in the home and her role was to complement and support the man of the house, avoiding intellectual occupations which could be detrimental to this role. (See Santovetti 396)

18 Interest in Neera's production is further documented by the publication in recent decades of many of her novels and theoretical volumes: *Una giovinezza del secolo XIX* (1975 and 1981), *Teresa* (1976, 1995, 2009, 2012), *Le idee di una donna* and *Confessioni letterarie* (1977), *Crepuscoli di libertà* (1977), *L'indomani* (1981), *Dizionario d'igiene per le famiglie* (1985), *Monastero e altri racconti* (1987), *Crevalcore* (1991 and 2009), *Un nido* (1994), *Lydia* (1997), *Il libro di mio figlio* (2012) and *Voci della notte* (2013 and 2017).

19 It is precisely women who are successful - and "respectful" - the spearheads of women's affirmation in literature, who prove to be ... hesitant and uncertain in drawing in theory the emancipationist and social consequences that would seem to be a logical consequence of the cases described in their narrative.

20 I will never belong to any school, I will never follow any method, I will always remain too realistic for one, too sentimental for the other. But since there is still someone who accepts me as I am, for those few I will continue to write - and even better than for those few, for the only divine one who inspires me - what, my friend, I can't call any other way: the ideal in reality.

References

Aleramo, Sibilla. *Una donna*. Milan, Feltrinelli, 1997.

Arslan, Antonia. *Dame, galline e regine. La scrittura femminile italiana fra '800 e '900*, edited by Marina Pasqui. Milan, Guerini, 1998.

———."Ideologia e autorappresentazione. Donne intellettuali fra Ottocento e Novecento." *Svelamento. Sibilla Aleramo: una biografia intellettuale*. Milan, Feltrinelli, 1998, pp. 164–177.

——— and Maria Grazia Raffaele, editors. *Fanfulla della domenica*. Treviso, Canova, 1981.

Baldacci, Luigi. Introduction. *Teresa*, by Neera. Turin, Einaudi, 1976, pp. v–xii.

Capuana, Luigi. *Studii sulla letteratura contemporanea*, edited by Paola Azzolini, Naples, Liguori, 1988.

Cavarero, Adriana. "Per una teoria della differenza sessuale." *Il Pensiero della differenza sessuale*. Diotima. Milan, Tartaruga, 1987, pp. 43–79.

Cixous, Hélène. "The Laugh of the Medusa," translated by Keith Cohen and Paula Cohen. *Signs*, vol. 1, no. 4, 1976, pp. 875–893.

Corda, Maria Grazia. *Il profumo della memoria. Identità e scrittura in Neera*. Florence, Atheneum, 1993.

Corti, Maria. "C'è un fantasma sotto lo scialle." *La Repubblica*, vol. 19, Mar. 19, 1992, p. 26.

Cousineau, Diane. *Letters and Labyrinths: Women Writing/Cultural Codes*. Newark, U of Delaware P, 1997.

Croce, Benedetto. *La letteratura della nuova Italia*. Bari, Laterza, 1948.

Irigaray, Luce. *Speculum of the Other Woman*, translated by Gillian C. Gill, Ithaca, Cornell UP, 1985.

Kroha, Lucienne. *The Woman Writer in Late 19th Century Italy: Gender and the Formation of Literary Identity*. Lewiston, Mellen, 1992.

Landes, Joan B., editor. *Feminism: The Public and the Private*. Oxford, Oxford UP, 1998.

Menasci, Guido. "Neera." *Nuova Antologia*, vol. 53, 1901, pp. 263–278.

Merry, Bruce. "Neera." *Italian Women Writers. A Bio-Bibliographical Sourcebook*, edited by Rinaldina Russell, London, Greenwood, 1994, pp. 286–294.

Mitchell, Katharine. *Italian Women Writers: Gender and Everyday Life in Fiction and Journalism, 1870–1910*. Toronto, U of Toronto P, 2014.

Momigliano, Anna. "'The Ferrante Effect': In Italy Women Writers are Ascendant." *The New York Times*, 9 December. 2019, https://www.nytimes.com/2019/12/09/books/elena-ferrante-italy-women-writers.html. Accessed 25 March, 2020.

Neera. *Addio*! 1877. Milan, Baldini & Castoldi, 1919.

———. *Confessioni letterarie*. 1891. *Neera*, edited by Benedetto Croce, Milan, Garzanti, 1942, pp. 871–809.

———. *Le idee di una donna*. 1903. *Neera*, edited by Benedetto Croce, Milan, Garzanti, 1942, pp. 777–867.

———. *Una giovinezza del secolo XIX*. Milan, Cogliati, 1919.

Nozzoli, Anna. *Tabù e coscienza. La condizione femminile nella letteratura italiana del Novecento*. Florence, Nuova Italia, 1978.

Pacifici, Sergio. *The Modern Italian Novel from Capuana to Tozzi*. Carbondale, Southern Illinois UP, 1973.

Santovetti, Olivia. "Neera (1846–1918). The World Seen from the Window: Reading, Writing, and the Power of Fantasy." *The Italianist*, vol. 33, no. 3, October 2012, pp. 388–402.

Sanvitale, Francesca, editor. *Invito alla lettura di Neera*. Florence, Vallecchi, 1977.

Serao, Matilde. *Ricordando Neera*. Milan, Treves, 1920.

Showalter, Elaine. *A Literature of Their Own: British Women Novelists from Bronte to Lessing*. Princeton, Princeton UP, 1977.

Spinazzola, Vittorio. "Introduzione a Neera." *Ritratto di signora. Neera (Anna Radius Zuccari) e il suo tempo*, edited by Antonia Arslan and Marina Pasqui, Milan, Guerini, 1999, pp. 11–12.

Trotta, Donatella, editor. *Album Serao*. Naples, Fiorentino, 1991.

Wood, Sharon. *Italian Women's Writing 1860–1994*. London, Athlone, 1995.

Zambon, Patrizia. "Leggere per scrivere. La Formazione autodidattica delle scrittrici tra Otto e Novecento: Neera, Ada Negri, Grazia Deledda, Sibilla Aleramo." *Studi Novecenteschi*, vol. 16, no. 38, 1989, pp. 287–324.

2 From Daughter to Mother in Neera's Work

Neera's early novels portray late nineteenth-century Italian women's limited existence within an oppressive society which obliges them to submit passively to social and cultural norms for female behavior or face the consequences if they transgress. Although Sandra Gilbert and Susan Gubar observe in *The Madwoman in the Attic: The Woman Writer and the Nineteenth Century Literary Imagination* (1979) the tendency among women writers of the period to create "works of fiction that subordinate other women by perpetuating a morality that sanctifies or vilifies all women into submission" (69), in *Figuring Women. A Thematic Study of Giovanni Verga's Female Characters* (2004), Susan Amatangelo suggests that such a binary portrayal of female reality was not limited only to women writers, noting a similar classification of Giovanni Verga's heroines "according to two common cultural types: the Angel of the Hearth, the bourgeois ideal of domestic femininity; and the Fatal Woman, a threat to domestic tranquility" (11). Novels by both female and male writers realistically reflecting women's limited options within society, channel women's options into a choice between acquiescence or infraction of society's unspoken rules for female conduct. Kroha interprets the adultery/punishment theme that dominates Neera's early work as serving a two-fold purpose for this writer: to avoid identification with her disobedient protagonists and simultaneously express the conflict of roles she herself experienced as writer and woman (71–72). I will show, in fact, that there exists an underlying tension in the early phase of Neera's career, starting with *Addio!* (1877) and culminating with the trilogy *Teresa* (1886), *Lydia* (1887) and *L'indomani* (1890), in the simultaneous adherence to and denunciation of patriarchal standards for female behavior. In "Neera (1846–1918). The World Seen from the Window: Reading, Writing, and the Power of Fantasy" (2012) Olivia Santovetti notes how Neera's privileging of the novel as genre of choice to explore the female oppressed condition lends itself to this dualistic objective because the novel "propagandizes a system of values in a different light; it compensates temporarily for the reader's dissatisfactions and on the other hand stirs up in the reader new desires, new dissatisfactions" (397).

Amatangelo notes the limited options for fulfillment for women of Neera's time: "Young women in Italy had few options as they approached adulthood; they could marry, take religious vows, or, possibly, remain in the family of origin in a caretaking capacity" (21). By portraying the restrictions women faced and the consequences deriving from failure to adhere to such restrictions, Neera calls attention to the plight of late nineteenth-century women and sets the stage already in her early novels for what she will later come to propose in her theoretical and later narrative production as the means for women's redemption: a female order that valorizes women's unique qualities. A progression can be traced in the development and evolution of Neera's female protagonists throughout her career, from oppressed daughter figures, trapped in unsatisfactory situations in which fulfillment eludes them, to redeemed mother figures who find gratification in the maternal role. Neera elevates maternity and the maternal instinct as a source of empowerment rather than inferiority for women, making her a point of reference for modern Italian feminist thought on the denigration of the feminine and the maternal within patriarchal society.

Neera's early novels demonstrate the lack of alternatives available for women of her time in achieving personal fulfillment: conformation to bourgeois codes of conduct, which often requires the sacrifice of happiness, or transgression of such codes, which frequently results in alienation or even death. The choices available to the protagonists of Neera's early novels can be seen to mirror her limited options as late nineteenth-century woman writer: conformation to male-dominated literary standards, in the creation of works that perpetuate accepted models of female behavior, or transgression of those standards in offering her characters the opportunity to fulfill themselves outside limited roles. In this phase of her career, Neera neither entirely conforms to nor transgresses traditional literary models, offering instead a "hidden" criticism, a technique not unusual for nineteenth-century women writers who, as Gilbert and Gubar note, often "created submerged meanings, meanings hidden within or behind the more accessible, 'public' content of their works, so that their literature could be read and appreciated even when its vital concern with female dispossession and disease was ignored" (72).

Neera's Daughters: *Addio!, Il castigo, Il marito dell'amica, La Regaldina, Teresa, Lydia and L'indomani*

In *Addio!* (1877), Neera's representation of the father-daughter relationship demonstrates the conditioning of female desire and aspirations as a result of the father's example and influence.[1] Throughout the novel, Valeria's deference to the authority of the paternal figure induces her to accept his teachings and repress her personal desires for fulfillment and sexual satisfaction. She vaunts her chaste reputation and infallible moral character, which she attributes to the influence of the example set by her father: "Figlia a un intemerato veterano delle patrie battaglie – glorioso soldato del ventuno e del quartantotto, campione di tutte le virtù – io crebbi come una giovane spartana, fra gli esempi di magnanimità e di valore" [Daughter to an honorable veteran of the fatherland's wars - glorious soldier of '21 and '48, champion of all virtues - I grew up as a young Spartan, among the examples of magnanimity and valor] (Neera, *Addio!* 13). Valeria marries Attilio, a much older friend of her father's, because of her respect and devotion for the paternal figure, and even after Attilio's death frees her from her marital obligations, she rejects an opportunity for passionate love with Massimo as opposed to the platonic love that had characterized her relationship with Attilio. It is interesting to note that Neera's portrayal of the father-daughter relationship is dynamic: Valeria aspires to follow the positive example set by her father, even though pursuing that choice entails the sacrifice of her own personal desires, revealing his influence as simultaneously oppressive in nature. Ultimately, Valeria chooses to leave her home and Massimo behind, rather than allow herself to succumb to her desire for a passionate kind of love. Valeria's self-imposed exile and resignation to a fate of negation and alienation exemplify her submission to a social order which does not recognize the possibility for female fulfillment outside of marriage. Neera's dedication to "donne oneste" [honest women] (*Addio!* 6) in the novel's original preface suggests, in fact, that the reward for women in adopting virtuous behavior is to be found in virtue itself. However, in the preface to *Addio!*'s third edition, Neera responds to criticism "per aver dato un carattere troppo sensuale a questo amore" [for having given a too sensual character to this love] (*Addio!* 9), defending her protagonist as "una vera donna di carne e di sangue" [a true woman of flesh and blood] (*Addio!* 8) and denouncing men's unwillingness to accept a representation of women contrary to patriarchal conceptions: "gli uomini, quasi esclusivamente, non vollero accettare questa donna diversa dalla donna che hanno fabbricato loro per proprio comodo" [men, almost exclusively, did not want to accept this woman different from the woman they made for their own convenience] (*Addio!* 8). Neera's comments from this later preface confirm the tension in this phase of her literary production between adhering to a culturally appropriate representation of female behavior and her awareness of its injustice.

Although Neera demonstrates in *Addio!* the pressure on women to negate their personal desires in order to follow the paternal example, she also suggests the idea, developed further in later novels, of the alternative offered by the maternal role. During her struggle between adhering to cultural norms and her desire for a sensual love, Valeria comes to recognize the maternal instinct as a source of redemption: "Benedite, o madri, i vostri dolori; benedite la fronte dei vostri bambini, sulla quale le vostre sante labbra potranno posarsi per sempre! Benedite l'amore legittimo, l'amore fecondo, l'amore imperituro! Perché, mio Dio, perché non fui madre?" [Bless, oh mothers, your sorrows; bless the forehead of your children, on which your holy lips may rest forever! Bless the legitimate love, the fruitful love, the everlasting love! Why, my God, why was I not a mother?] (Neera, *Addio!* 62). Ultimately, the novel proposes the maternal model over the paternal one as capable of offering women fulfillment, providing an important example in this early phase of Neera's career of her attention to a theme that would come to dominate her later literary and theoretical production.

In *Il castigo* (The punishment, 1881) Neera again explores the limited options for fulfillment often encountered by women of her time, in this case the option between spinsterhood or accepting a marriage of convenience. Temptation and yearning for passionate love are the dominant themes, but in this novel, the protagonist succumbs to her desire, only to later pay a high price for her transgression. Spinsterhood is presented in this novel as a fate to be avoided at any cost and one which can even bring about physically negative consequences: hysteria. Neera suggests the cause for Laura's hysteria in the cultural norms and social pressure that present marriage as the only form of fulfillment for women. Amatangelo notes: "For women in the 1800s, marriage was considered a social necessity since it offered them an identity in the world, a social dignity they could not otherwise achieve" (44). Neera describes the hysterical attacks which afflict Laura before her decision to accept a marriage of convenience as "isterismi di zitella" hysterical attacks of a spinster] (*Il castigo* 55) and presents her repressed fantasies as triggering her hysterical attacks. Neera's portrayal of Laura's hysteria reflects a Freudian understanding of hysterical fantasies as the "representation – the realization – of a phantasy with a sexual content" (Freud, *Dora* 39).[2] Laura's body, the body of the spinster, rebels against sexual dissatisfaction and repression through hysterical attacks. Neera's portrayal of the spinster's psychological and physical suffering reveals her attention to this important but often overlooked social issue for women of her time. In her essay "The Spinster in the Works of Neera and Matilde Serao: Other or Mother?" (2013), Lucy Hosker notes the social marginality of the figure of the spinster, who was "a by-product of a society that required women to respect a certain model of behavior, sanctioned by its cultural longevity, and founded on the principles of obedience and submission to male authority" (67).

Having accepted a marriage of convenience with a man she does not love, Laura later gives in to her desire for love by having an affair with another man. Laura finds fulfillment not in this physical love but in the love for the daughter born from her affair. As in *Addio!*, Neera suggests maternal love as an ideal form of love, capable of offering women a fulfillment otherwise unobtainable: "Il sentimento materno è così completo, così potente che abbraccia tutto dal grandissimo al piccolissimo." [The maternal feeling is so complete, so powerful that it embraces everything from the very large to the very small] (Neera, *Il castigo* 59). However, with the daughter's premature death due to illness and the exclamation by Laura's husband, who knows the truth, that "[i]l castigo è tremendo" [punishment is fearsome] (Neera, *Il castigo* 84), Neera suggests the daughter's death is the price Laura must pay for seeking to fulfill her desire for physical love. It is interesting to note that in *Confessioni letterarie*, Neera refers to Laura as a victim of society's "grande ingiustizia" [great injustice], offering the following explanation: "la società, che priva le donne dei loro diritti naturali ove non abbiano trovato un marito, si fa poi beffe di loro se rimangono zitelle, e le chiama maligne, invidiose, sensuali" [society, which deprives women of their natural rights if they have not found a husband, then mocks them if they remain spinsters, and calls them malignant, envious, sensual] (872). Although Neera recognizes the injustice of Laura's situation in the context of her autobiographical writing, the novel's justice exacts its revenge on Laura for her transgression, offering another example of the tension in this early phase of Neera's career.

In *Il marito dell'amica* (1884) and *La Regaldina* (1885), Neera adopts a dualistic portrayal of women in the representation of moral and submissive heroines and their rebellious and sensual counter-heroines. In *Il marito dell'amica,* Neera contrasts the aspirations for fulfillment of two friends, the moral heroine Maria and the superficial counter-heroine Sofia, in a story of adulterous temptation that culminates in renunciation and alienation. After two experiences of disappointment in love, the contemplative Maria does not surrender to feelings of bitterness, deriving instead from those experiences a source of strength and growth of character. Similar to the familial relationships presented in *Addio!* and Neera's autobiographical writings, Maria's strength of character is linked to the influence of the paternal figure, who provides the moral guidance for the daughter's development, while the mother is absent. The shallow Sofia, on other hand, unsatisfied with her husband whom she describes as cold and distant, accepts as an illusion her dreams of finding love and passion within marriage, consoling herself instead with the attention she receives from other men: "Pensare che noi tutte si cresce nella speranza di un amore unico, immenso, potente, eterno; che a questa chimera dedichiamo il meglio delle nostre aspirazioni e che alla fine; tutte, qual più... qual meno... ci tocca prendere due o tre corteggiatori per compensarci dell'amore che non c'è" [To think that we all grow up in the hope of a unique, immense, powerful, eternal love; that we dedicate the best of our aspirations to this chimera and that in the end, all of us, who more... who less... have to take two or three suitors to compensate us for the love that is not there"] (Neera, *Il marito dell'amica* 20–21). Neera again offers a critique of bourgeois marriage, portraying it as a compromise for women and revealing the disillusionment that accompanies female awareness. As in *Addio!,* Maria rejects the temptation of physical love, presented by the advances of Sofia's husband, choosing instead to alienate herself from home and friends to avoid the temptation of an affair.

In *La Regaldina*, Neera juxtaposes the virtuous and sacrificing Daria to the sensual and adulterous Matilde to again contrast a model of female submission to one of female transgression. Whereas Daria resigns herself to not being able to share a life with the man she loves, Matilde's brother Ippolito, for familial obligations and economic reasons, Matilde compromises herself with

Daria's brother Rodolfo for a night of passion. Although a quickly arranged marriage saves both families' honor, Matilde and Rodolfo do not love each other and Matilde takes little interest in caring for their child, leaving Daria to fulfill the maternal role. Unsatisfied with her marriage and bored by domestic life, Matilde begins an affair with another man. When she discovers that he plans to marry another woman, however, Matilde kills herself, leaving behind her husband and two young children, all of whom Daria takes on the duty of caring for. Through Daria, Neera reveals patriarchal society's expectations of women: serve and love others, placing one's aspirations for love and personal fulfillment second to familial needs, without expecting or requiring to be loved in return. Similar to *Addio!* and *Il marito di un'amica*, the heroine's virtue is to be her only reward, while alienation and, in this case, death await those women who do not resign themselves to the submissive role reserved for them by society. Neera juxtaposes bourgeois notions of acceptability for female roles, the submissive and selfless wife and mother, to the socially unacceptable woman who seeks her own fulfillment. As in previous novels, Daria also finds fulfillment in the maternal role, as she explains to Ippolito, "Io sarò sempre felice finchè avrò un dovere da compiere e degli esseri da amare" [I will always be happy as long as I have a duty to fulfill and people to love] (Neera, *La Regaldina* 165). While the maternal role is present also in this novel as a possible source of fulfillment for women, Neera focuses more attention in this novel on the choices women face within society which attempts to categorize them as saints or sinners.

Neera's criticism of the cultural norms and social restrictions that govern women's lives and limit their opportunities for happiness and fulfillment reaches a peak with the trilogy of novels *Teresa, Lydia* and *L'indomani*, which represent a turning point in her career for the realism with which she portrays situations of female dissatisfaction and for the denunciatory tone with which she inculpates the society of her time.

Teresa is the story of the daughter's oppression in late nineteenth-century patriarchal Italy as well as the social analysis of the "problema della donna che rimane nubile" [problem of the woman who remains unmarried] (*Una giovinezza* 213), as Neera reveals in her autobiography. The novel narrates a reality common to many young middle-class women of the day, whose aspirations were cut short by familial needs and concerns. Amatangelo notes the limited choices for women of the time regarding their options in choosing whom to marry: "Leading up to marriage, the fundamental issue of choosing a mate brings to light the woman's lack of power; the selection of a husband was not her own, but the responsibility of her family, and she was expected to comply with its will" (44). When her father refuses to grant her a dowry, because the money is destined for financing her brother's studies, Teresa confronts the reality that economic factors deny her the right to marry the man she loves. Refusing a marriage of convenience, she remains within her home as family caretaker, hoping that one day Orlandi's financial circumstances will allow them to marry. With this novel, Neera exposes and ultimately denounces the social structures that limit women's possibilities for personal fulfillment to marriage, often one of convenience, observing in *Teresa*: "Quale infame ingiustizia pesa dunque ancora sulla nostra società, che si chiama incivilita, se una fanciulla deve scegliere tra il ridicolo della verginità e la vergogna del matrimonio di convenienza?" [What infamous injustice still weighs on our society, which claims itself civilized, if a woman has to choose between the ridicule of virginity and the shame of a marriage of convenience?] (180). Teresa's situation, limited by familial expectations and circumstances, recalls that of other female protagonists of the period: for example, the protagonist of Giovanni Verga's *Storia di una capinera* (Story of a blackcap), who is forced into a convent, or *I Malavoglia*'s Mena, whose poverty also limits her options for marriage.

Similar to *Il castigo*'s Laura, Teresa also suffers from hysteria because of her unfulfilled desire for love. Her body rebels against the passing of her youth and beauty, and her first hysterical episode occurs after someone refers to her as a *zitellona* [spinster]. Teresa's hysterical episodes continue throughout the novel, coinciding with significant occasions, such as the wedding day of her younger twin sisters, the moment that ultimately confirms her fate as spinster. Teresa hides her yearning for love, overcome by feelings of shame and by her fear of discovery. Elaine Showalter notes in *A Literature of Their Own* (1977) that social customs instructed women to hide femininity and female physical experience as something of which to be ashamed (81). Teresa carries guilt not only for her resistance to her father's wishes, in continuing to love Orlandi in secret, but also for her yearning for love: "Aveva la persuasione di amare troppo, più assai che non sia permesso dalla religione e dal pudore femminile" [She felt that she loved too much, more so than was permitted by religion and female modesty] (Neera, *Teresa* 154). Teresa's hysteria represents the unconscious expression of her repressed desire, but at the same time the disease also constitutes the means by which she is able to subtract herself from familial expectations. Through her hysterical attacks, in fact, Teresa is no longer the self-sacrificing daughter. In *The Female Malady* (1985), Showalter discusses hysteria as the means for nineteenth-century women to break out of the selfless roles enforced upon them by noting that when the hysterical woman is sick "she demand[s] service and attention from others" (133). Neera blames Teresa's fate and condition on the "fathers" of the society that determine women's role and opportunities:

> [Teresa] Capiva le ragioni del padre: aveva troppo vissuto in quell'ambiente e in quello solo, per non essere persuasa che la sua condizione di donna le imponeva anzitutto la rassegnazione al suo destino, - un destino ch'ella non era libera di dirigere – che doveva accettare così come le giungeva, mozzato dalle esigenze della famiglia, sottoposto ai bisogni e ai desideri degli altri. (*Teresa* 170)[3]

Denouncing Teresa's "condition as woman" as that which restricts her options for fulfillment in society, Neera identifies the source of Teresa's hysteria in the conflict between natural impulses and social constraints.

Teresa conducts a suffocated existence within the confines of the family home, the spaces of which delimit those areas intended for women, such as the small room where Teresa and her mother carry out their daily activities, and those reserved for men, such as the study inhabited only by the father and son. In "La narrativa realista nei romanzi d'autrice di fine Ottocento," (Realist fiction in turn-of-the-century novels, 1997) Patrizia Zambon notes the similarities between *Teresa* and the novel *Un matrimonio in provincia* (A small-town marriage) by Marchesa Colombi, written the year before Neera's novel in 1885, in the narration of the daily lives of the female protagonists during their long wait for love: "La vita che vi è narrata si muove tutto nella pacata normalità di un'educazione domestica" [The life that is narrated moves in the calm normality of a domestic education] (170). Teresa's life plays out within the home, and she observes the external world as an outsider, through the grates of the window when she secretly meets Orlandi. As in many of Neera's novels, familial relations constitute an integral part of the female protagonist's domestic reality, shaping and limiting her choices and options for fulfillment. Signor Caccia's oppressive and dominating personality contrasts with the passive and submissive character of Teresa's mother, while the juxtaposition between

Teresa and her brother is especially striking since he is allowed access to the world from which Teresa is excluded and also the freedom to choose whom to marry.

Not surprisingly, it is only her father's death that frees Teresa from her daughterly duties, allowing her in the conclusion of the novel to leave home and finally join Orlandi, now ill and needing help. Teresa's "liberation" is quite limited, as she herself acknowledges when she justifies her decision to her only remaining friend: "Ebbene, dirai ai zelanti che ho pagato con tutta la mia vita questo momento di libertà. È abbastanza caro nevvero?" [Well, you will tell the zealots that I have paid for this moment of freedom with all my life. It's quite costly isn't it?] (Neera, *Teresa* 202). Amatangelo notes, regarding Verga's portrayal of female adolescence, that "the clash between a young woman's search for identity and the expectations of nineteenth-century Italian society ends with the defeat of the young woman" (42). Many critics perceive the ending of *Teresa* as a defeat for this protagonist. Baldacci observes regarding the novel's conclusion: "Questa seconda vita di Teresa, in cui trionferà l'ideale, possiamo anche immaginarcela come verosimile, ma artisticamente vera è sola la sua prima vita: cioè il romanzo – meno due pagine – che abbiamo sott'occhio" [We can also imagine this second life of Teresa's, in which the ideal triumphs, as plausible, but only her first life is artistically true: that is, the novel - minus two pages - that we have before us] (xi). The novel's ending, however, represents the end of Teresa's long-awaited idealized life with Orlandi and the beginning of the real one. Zambon confirms the importance of the protagonist's final gesture: "Agire invece di sognare" [act instead of dream] (170). Although a victim for many years of society's restrictions for women, Teresa is not fully defeated in that she finally escapes the confines of the family home.

In *Lydia*, Neera explores the options for female fulfillment within the high ranks of society. Lydia is a young, wealthy aristocrat who possesses a substantial dowry for securing her future marriage. In this novel Neera reveals the difficulty also for women of elevated social status to avoid social, economic and familial limitations and marry according to their personal aspirations. Whereas familial and economic restrictions limit Teresa's options for marriage, Lydia is restricted in her choices because of the influence of her wealth upon her suitors: "Noi, nel nostro mondo reale, abbiamo degli scioperati che vagheggiano i nostri denari senza neppure conoscere il colore dei nostri occhi" [In our real world, we have deadbeats that desire our money without even knowing the color of our eyes]

(Neera, *Lydia* 63). Giuliana Morandini notes the following similarity between the protagonists of the two novels: "Teresa e Lydia sono due esempi di donne che cercano con tutte le forze di realizzarsi, senza isolarsi e senza accettare compromessi" [Teresa and Lydia are two examples of women who try with all their strength to fulfill themselves, without isolating themselves and without making compromises] (16). The protagonists of the two novels are two women who struggle against adverse forces to obtain fulfillment and happiness, each within their own social class and familial setting. Lydia reveals the necessary qualities a woman of her social standing must possess in order to achieve her objectives:

> [Lydia] Aveva compreso subito, fin dalla prima comparsa in società, il posto importante che vi tiene la donna abile, scaltra, senza scrupoli, elegante e procace. Solamente nella sua smania di afferrare questo vero per trarne profitto, trascurò una osservazione principalissima: non tenne conto dell'immenso divario che corre fra la donna maritata e la zitella: tutto ciò che è permesso alla prima, tutto ciò che si vieta alla seconda. Credette che il suo ingegno e la sua ricchezza bastassero a darle l'indipendenza, reputandosi assai forte per vincere pregiudizi secolari. (Neera, *Lydia* 111)[4]

Lydia naively seeks out an independence which not even her wealth can obtain for her. Although she possesses a substantial dowry, she is nonetheless susceptible to the same conditions as Teresa that govern women's options for fulfillment in society: marriage or a non-existence. The novel reveals the fate of an unmarried woman, even the aristocratic wealthy one, in turn-of-the-century Italian society: "Così la donna sola; fra gli strati bassi dell'intelligenza e del sentire assomiglia ai crostacei; nella condizione di Lydia è un'ermafrodita" [Thus the single woman; among the low levels of intelligence and feeling, resembles crustaceans; in Lydia's condition she is a hermaphrodite] (Neera, *Lydia* 243). In comparing the status of the unmarried refined, aristocratic woman to a biological rarity, Neera reveals the limited options for also women of Lydia's elevated social class outside of marriage. To have a role within society, women must be married or face social alienation.

In *Lydia*, Neera exposes the artistocratic woman's struggle for self-fulfillment as limited also by social conceptions of femininity. Taking as her motto "divertirsi!" [have fun!] (Neera, *Lydia* 186), Lydia conducts a superficial existence, caught up in social appearances and flirting with men until such a lifestyle becomes an inescapable reality. Having grown up concerned only with stylish clothes and physical beauty, when Lydia discovers the first signs of her aging body, she questions the sense of such an existence that is destined to pass quickly. In the article "Femminile plurale" [Female pluralities] published in *Fanfulla della domenica* one year before *Lydia*, Neera objects to the predominant portrayal within society of women as "a semplice strumento di piacere" [simple instrument of pleasure]:

> Noi vediamo donne dappertutto. Non si pubblica un libro, uno spartito, un programma, che non abbiano nel frontispizio una procace figura femminile, quasi sempre nuda. Le vetrine dei cartolai riboccano di fotografie di donne. La fortuna dei teatri riposa sulle donne. I giornali più serii dedicano al bel sesso cronachette della moda e registrano i trionfi delle *professional beauties*. Infine, ogni uomo ha nel taschino la scatola dei fiammiferi con due tipi di donna, la bionda e la bruna; ma in tanta abbondanza di donne, la donna si perde. (qtd. Arslan and Raffaele 168)[5]

Neera criticizes, both within her narrative and journalistic production, society's widespread objectification of women for their physical attributes. *Lydia*'s conclusion offers a grim prospective on women's chances for avoiding objectification and social pressures to fulfill certain roles. Discovering shortly before her wedding day that her fiancé is her friend's lover and that he only wants to marry her for her money, Lydia kills herself, revealing first to a friend: "Perché dovrei lottare? Non ho nessun ideale che mi sostenga; non ho nemmeno più la possibilità di godere, perché, guardi, i capelli bianchi incominciano…" [Why should I fight? I don't have any ideal to support me; I don't even have the chance for pleasure anymore, because, look, I'm getting grey hair...] (Neera, *Lydia* 186). Lydia acknowledges and succumbs to the pressure on women to adhere to traditional standards linked to female youth and beauty. Reflecting the stylistic objectives of this novel, faithful to *verismo* and its objective portrayal of reality, as will be discussed further in the following chapter, with *Lydia* Neera brings attention to another facet of female reality of her time, this time within the upper-class sphere.

L'indomani explores the oppressed female condition within marriage, criticizing the way bourgeois society "prepares" women for wifedom with false expectations. Following the stories of a spinster's hysteria and a single woman's suicide in *Teresa* and *Lydia*, Neera suggests in this concluding novel of her trilogy that women are unable to find happiness and fulfillment even within marriage. Amatangelo notes that although "young women theoretically improved their position through matrimony, in effect they moved into a realm governed by tradition and rigid ideas regarding the female destiny" (44). The novel opens with the female protagonist Marta's sense of surprise, the morning after her wedding to Alberto, at finding herself in the same room and bed with a man she has known for only two months. Marta's marriage is one of convenience, and the novel recounts her decision to marry Alberto, one of many suitors presented by her mother when she reached the age to marry, based on various factors such as age, status, economic stability and appearance. Marta's unsatisfied dreams of marital bliss deriving from passionate love quickly lead to the realization that marital life does not correspond to her fantasies. Amatangelo notes that "[a]fter marriage, brides were expected to embody the Angel of the Hearth, the wifely ideal promoted by nineteenth-century Western culture" (44). *L'indomani* confirms such expectations through the advice Marta receives from a friend regarding the reality of marriage for women:

> Per le donne oneste ... l'amore non può essere che un dovere o un peccato; un contratto stipulato, firmato, reso sacramento, reso dovere civile, eguagliato all'ordine sacro o alla vendita di un podere; oppure uno strappo alle convenienze, alle leggi, alla religione, all'onore. (*L'indomani* 47–48)[6]

Neera criticizes the patriarchal categorization of love for women as either duty or sin and the manipulation of women within a social system that prepares them, to the sole advantage of men, for the role of caretaker within marriage.

Unsatisfied in her marriage, Marta is another daughter figure who remains in a state of sexual immaturity and frustration, yet her body, like that of Teresa and Lydia, demands attention and love. Paola Azzolini suggests in "*Lydia* o la tentazione della scrittura" (*Lydia* or the temptation of writing, 1999) that this novel demonstrates "la forza e la presenza del corpo femminile, il corpo della donna che ha bisogno dell'amore e della maternità, pena la consunzione, la malattia, l'emarginazione triste delle zitelle o la fine violenta delle sognatrici ribelli come Lydia" [the strength and presence of the female body, the body of the woman in need of love and motherhood, which results in exhaustion, illness, the sad marginalization of spinsters or the violent end of rebel dreamers like Lydia] (23). Often alone at home in the evening and overcome by feelings of solitude, Marta fantasizes a passionate kind of love. Her desire for sensual love manifests itself during these moments alone which provide occasion for sexual self-pleasuring:

> Il tempo passava, e dall'immobilità angosciosa Marta entrava in uno stato di allucinazione sensuale. Con mano inconscia slacciava i ganci dell'abito, allentava i nastri, cedendo a una sensazione misteriosa di abbandono, con dei brividi a fior di pelle, la bocca assetata, arida, le braccia aperte disperatamente. … Perduta nelle immagini d'amore scioglieva i capelli, e attorcigliandoseli sul volto ne aspirava l'aroma giovanile, gemendo il proprio nome – Marta, Marta! … Il tempo passava ancora, finché l'eccitazione illanguidendosi la lasciava sfinita, con le membra rotte, gli occhi pesti e vacillanti. (Neera, *L'indomani* 75)[7]

The above passage reveals Neera's sensibility as a woman writer attentive to the dissatisfaction and yearnings of women of her time who are denied an outlet for their sexual desires. Marta remains in a state of sexual frustration due to the repression of her desire and her husband's inability and unwillingness to comprehend it. Mitchell suggests in "Neera's refiguring of hysteria as *nervosismo*" (2010) that the fact that Marta "explore[s] self-love through the imaginary while alone is revealing not only of the protagonist's desire for intimacy with a man and women's unsatisfied erotic drives, but is also illustrative of the protagonist's sense of powerlessness" (112). Neera expertly portrays the frustration of Marta's situation, frustrated and desperate for love but unable to live out her sexuality outside of her fantasies.

L'indomani's conclusion consolidates Neera's views, anticipated in many of her previous novels, on the need for a new order that values the maternal. In the end of the novel, in fact, it is Marta's mother who comforts and advises Marta, who is now pregnant, on a different kind of love, helping her to recognize the strength and importance of the maternal instinct: "Sentiva la sue viscere commoversi sotto un impulso di persona viva, colla strana rivelazione di un altro essere in se stessa. Sembrava una piccola mano che battesse contro il suo seno, una piccola mano che voleva dire: Aprimi, io sono l'amore e la verità" [She felt her bowels moving under an impulse of a living person, with the strange revelation of another being in herself. It seemed like a small hand beating against her breast, a small hand that wanted to say: Open me, I am love and truth] (Neera, *L'indomani* 142–143).[8] Ultimately Marta finds fulfillment in the notion that she is part of a higher order, that of life's productive cycle: "Tutto muore, tutto nasce, tutto cambia, tutto si rinnova, le tombe scoperchiate servono di culla, i cuori insanguinati e piangenti danno nuovo sangue e nuove lagrime alla vita" [Everything dies, everything is born, everything changes, everything is renewed, the uncovered graves serve as a cradle, the bloody and weeping hearts give new blood and new tears to life] (Neera, *L'indomani* 144). Through the comforting figure of the mother and Marta's newfound sense of gratification, Neera proposes a maternal order based on the recognition of the dignity and fulfillment offered by the maternal mission and the transmission from generation to generation of the mother's wisdom. In "Maternal Prescriptions and Descriptions in Post-Unification Italy" (2013), Ursula Fanning notes regarding *L'indomani*'s connection between mother-daughter-unborn child that "Neera foreshadows here Kristeva's generational linking of (herself, her own mother and her son, peacefully physically intertwined) in 'Stabat Mater'" (21). Marta is the last of Neera's daughters, forced into passive acceptance of society's restrictive models for women, and the first of her "new women" protagonists who recognize the value and worth of their womanhood. Luisa Muraro affirms in *L'ordine simbolico della madre* (The symbolic maternal order, 1991) that women cannot achieve true freedom unless they comprehend the symbolic significance of the mother's power (9). The fulfillment that Marta finds in maternity at the end of the novel foreshadows the exaltation of uniquely female qualities that will dominate Neera's narrative and theoretical production from that point onward.

Motherhood and the Maternal in Neera's Theoretical Production

Neera's exaltation of the maternal role and instinct in the second half of her literary career develops from her awareness, demonstrated in her early production, of society's oppression and objectification of women. In her theoretical works *Il libro di mio figlio* (My son's book, 1891), *Battaglie per un'idea* (1898) and *Le idee di una donna* (1903), Neera suggests the recognition and appreciation of the maternal role and instinct as capable of redeeming and empowering women,[9] while she also explores the theme in her narrative production of the same years, in novels such as *L'amuleto* (The amulet, 1897), *La vecchia casa* (The old house, 1900), *Il romanzo della fortuna* (The novel of fortune, 1906) and *Duello d'anime* (Battle of souls, 1911). Neera reappropriates the maternal instinct from positivist discourse, which posits it as the basis for women's inferiority within society. In "A Modern Feminist Reading of the Maternal Instinct in Neera" (2010), I propose Neera as "a point of reference within the context of fin-de-siècle Italy for modern Italian feminist thought on the denigration of the feminine and the maternal within the paternal order of patriarchal society" (51).

Neera defends her views publicly on the pages of some of the period's leading journals. On more than one occasion in her journalistic production, she responds publicly and directly to Cesare Lombroso's affirmations regarding the inferiority of the female nature. Following the publication of a series of articles by Lombroso in the years 1892–93 in *L'Idea Liberale*,[10] Neera responds with a series of articles in which she criticizes the anthropologist's affirmations and proposes her own view of women's role in society.[11] In "Osservazioni" (Observations) for example, Neera sarcastically undermines scientific claims for women's inferiority based on evidence such as female insensitivity. She criticizes the methodology that produced such conclusions, based on evidence such as inferior brain weight and lack of modesty in women, and attacks the positivist's argument at its foundation, pointing to the unfounded and pseudo-scientific nature of the evidence used to support his claims. In "Femminismo storico" (Historical feminism), Neera criticizes biological superiority or inferiority among men and women as a scientifically unfounded idea:

> Là, là, le conosco le opinioni del signor Lombroso sulla pretesa inferiorità della donna, ma sono persuasa che in fondo non ci crede neppure lui. Come può un naturalista ammettere che servendosi dei medesimi mezzi si mettano al mondo alternativamente esseri superiori ed esseri inferiori? Si potrebbe crederlo, forse, se i maschi li facessero gli uomini. (*Le idee di una donna* 837)[12]

Neera sarcastically negates the validity of such theories as socially constructed notions propagated by men.

Above all, Neera's rejection of the notion of female inferiority derives from her ideal of men and women's corresponding roles, articulated around the concept that the two form a unit: "Veramente sarebbe da intaccare il principio nelle sue radici e chiedere come mai si possono considerare sotto due diversi aspetti le due parti di un solo e intimo tutto; fare una questione di razza dove è solo una questione di sesso" [Actually it would be necessary to undermine the principle at its roots and ask why it is possible to consider under two different aspects the two parts of a one and intimate whole; to make a matter of race where it is only a matter of sex] (*Battaglie* 121). Throughout her theoretical and narrative production, Neera argues that man and woman form a unit, neither one superior nor inferior. In the article "Il nodo della questione" (The crux of the matter), she criticizes the feminist goal of achieving equality with men, whether it be in competing for work or comparing brain size: "V'è alcuno che creda seriamente essere un bisogno della donna quella di eguagliare l'uomo, di fargli concorrenza, di provare che il peso dei loro cervelli è assolutamente eguale, o quanto mai, che la qualità compensa la quantità? Eh via!" [Is there anyone who seriously believes that a woman needs to equal man, to compete with him, to prove that the weight of their brains is absolutely equal, or even more, that quality compensates quantity? Come on!] (*Battaglie* 74). Neera's feminism is based on women's recognition of their unique qualities and individual worth, as she reveals in the article "Dei rapporti superiori fra l'uomo e la donna" (On the superior relations between men and women): "Il progresso che ora si apre alla donna e che l'ulcerata anima umana le chiede sperando, è un progresso tutto morale, tutto intimo" [The progress that is now available to women and that the ulcerated human soul asks of her hopefully, is a completely moral, intimate progress] (*Battaglie* 53–54). The possibility for female empowerment proposed by Neera did not correspond to that advanced by turn-of-the-century feminists who demanded the right to vote and access to education and professions, but rather it was based on promoting women's unique role in society.

In the 1903 volume *Le idee di una donna*, a collection of 15 articles dedicated to women's issues published originally for the most part in the journal *Il Marzocco*, Neera expounds her views on women's role in society. In the volume's preface, she expresses her opinion of the contemporary Italian feminist movement, which she criticizes as too masculine in nature to be true feminism, and offers instead her own version of feminism:

> È troppo maschile per essere del femminismo sincero. Gli sforzi che si fanno per uguagliare l'uomo mostrano chiaramente che la donna non si riconosce più nella integrità del

> proprio valore, ed è questo valore suo che difendo con schietto ardore, dedicando i miei sforzi alle donne che accettano con semplicità e nobilmente la loro grande missione, facendo cioè del femminismo vero. (*Le idee di una donna* 779–780)[13]

In articles such as "Guerra di sesso" (Battle of the sexes), "La Parte della donna" (The woman's part), "Femminismo storico" (Historical feminism), "Attività femminile" (Female activities), "Uomini, uomini, donne, donne" (Men, men, women, women) and "Tutte madri" (All mothers), Neera defends women's worth within society, exalting the maternal instinct and role as capable of differentiating women within patriarchal society and providing them the opportunity for social redemption and empowerment. Arguing in "La Parte della donna," for example, that women degrade themselves by performing men's duties in society, Neera claims: "Imitare e sostituire l'uomo mi sembra, oltre che inutile, molto più umiliante dell'avere una missione a sè, che la donna ha davvero ed infinitamente superiore a quelle che può togliere all'uomo" [Imitating and replacing men seems to me, besides being useless, much more humiliating than having a mission of one's own, which women really have and infinitely superior to that she can take away from men] (*Le idee di una donna* 801). Neera's rejection of female adherence to the male model reveals a consciousness that is neither reactionary nor aimed at supporting patriarchal oppression of women. In the article "Il Concetto materialistico della felicitià" (The materialistic concept of happiness), Neera recognizes the underlying risks for women in the new social system proposed by the turn-of-the-century feminist movement: "In realtà il femminismo non esiste. Esistono delle questioni economiche e morali che interessano in egual modo i due sessi" [In reality, feminism does not exist. There are economic and moral issues of equal interest to both sexes] (*Le idee di una donna* 784). As noted before, Neera's feminism represents a different type of progress for women, one that was intimate and moral (*Battaglie* 53–54).

Throughout her theoretical production, Neera develops her ideas on an ideal form of social conduct for men and women based on respect and love for each other, which includes respect for one's natural roles and duties. In the articles collected in *Le idee di una donna*, she expounds her ideas on the scientific foundations governing the fact that men and women each have certain duties:

> Formati fisiologicamente in modo diverso, hanno ricevuto dalla natura stessa il compito di differenti funzioni vitali; e dal

> momento che nessun progresso di civiltà farà di un uomo una madre, non c'è ragione nè materiale nè morale che le donne si assoggettino al tirocinio delle occupazioni maschili. (860)[14]

Neera classifies, therefore, the male model as a form of oppression for women, proposing instead sexual difference: "Né inferiori, né superiori, né uguali, ma diversi ed equivalenti" [Neither inferior, nor superior, nor equal, but different and equivalent] (*Le idee di una donna* 816). She proposes sexual difference by recognizing men and women's separate qualities and functions in society. Neera's representation of women's oppression within the paternal order of patriarchal society and the redemption offered by the maternal instinct make her a point of reference for modern feminist thought on sexual difference and the symbolic maternal order. Her understanding of sexual difference is aimed at protecting women from an equality which would ultimately result in women doing their work as well as that of men: "chi ha da perdere è la donna, perché oltre alle occupazioni, ai doveri, alle fatiche, ai dolori del suo sesso, dovrà aggiungervi le occupazioni, i doveri, le fatiche, i dolori dell'uomo" [it is the woman who stands to lose, because in addition to the occupations, duties, labors, pains of her sex, she will have to add also the occupations, duties, labors, pains of men] (*Le idee di una donna* 818). Literary critics such as Luigi Baldacci, Francesca Sanvitale and Edoardo Sanguineti have noted Neera's foresight in recognizing the risks for women in industrial society.[15] Baldacci notes, for example, that Neera "dimostra qualche intuizione non banale quando nel principio d'uguaglianza assunto dal femminismo vede il riflesso pratico dell'era industriale e dell'irreggimentazione della donna perseguita sotto il falso scopo dell'indipendenza economica" [demonstrates a non-trivial intuition when she views in the principle of equality asserted by feminism the practical reflection of the industrial age and the regimentation of women pursued under the false purpose of economic independence] (vii).

Modern feminist theorists such as Luce Irigaray[16] and Carla Lonzi[17] also claim sexual difference based on respect and admiration for men and women's respective roles in society. In her 1970 *Manifesto di rivolta femminile* (Manifest of female revolt), Lonzi states, "La donna non va definita in rapporto all'uomo. Su questa coscienza si fondano tanto la nostra lotta quanto la nostra libertà" [Woman is not to be defined in relation to man. All our struggle and freedom is based on this awareness] (*Sputiamo su Hegel* 11). In the essays collected in *Le idee di una donna*, Neera discourages women from competing with men for their professions, encouraging them instead to recognize the importance of their unique mission. The similarity of ideas on sexual difference reveals a common understanding of women's oppression within patriarchal society and the need to affirm women's individuality and personal worth as a way of empowerment.

Feminists in the Libreria delle Donne di Milano (Milan Feminist Bookstore Collective) and the Veronese feminist philosophical group Diotima have explored a feminist alternative to the sexist structures of patriarchal society by rejecting the Freudian interpretation of familial relations and reexamining the mother-daughter relationship as a way of recovering the mother as a positive figure within familial and social structures. The Milan Feminist Bookstore Collective volume *Non credere di avere dei diritti* (Don't believe you have rights, 1987) proposes a female order that exalts women's qualities and capabilities in contrast to the existing male order, which negates those qualities and capabilities. The notion of *affidamento* [fostering] between women, in the recognition of what women can offer each other, is suggested as a way of establishing a female order: "Affidarsi a una propria simile spesso, se non sempre, è indispensabile a una donna per raggiungere un fine sociale" [Relying on another similar to oneself is often, if not always, indispensable for a woman to achieve a social goal] (Libreria delle Donne di Milano 18). Rebecca West refers to relationships of *affidamento* as

> processes of mediation whereby more experienced and more authoritative women provide female modes of access to the world and to effective agency for their less experienced and usually younger 'affidate,' thus seeking to nullify the more deleterious effects of patriarchal power-based modes of mediation which do not take into account sexual difference. (210)

Neera proposes a maternal order for women that relies principally on women's recognition of their worth, but also on the transmission of such awareness from an experienced woman to a less experienced woman, as demonstrated through the mother-daughter relationship in the novel *L'indomani.*

In *L'ordine simbolico della madre* (1991), Luisa Muraro posits an alternative to the male order in a maternal genealogy, a "continuum materno" [maternal continuum] between women, be it symbolic or biological, as a way of fostering new and constructive relationships between women: "per la sua esistenza libera una donna ha bisogno, simbolicamente, della potenza materna" [for her free existence a woman needs, symbolically, the maternal power] (9). Muraro suggests that knowing how to love the mother, whose example has been rejected by patriarchal society, gives woman a true sense of being and represents "la possibilità di un altro ordine simbolico che non spoglia la madre delle sue qualità" [the possibility of another symbolic order that does not strip the mother of her qualities] (11). Neera also proposes a symbolic maternal order, given that her understanding of women's maternal mission is not tied exclusively to the reproductive function, as the following passage from *Le idee di una donna* reveals: "Siate madri. Se il vostro fianco non ha partorito fra i dolori il figlio delle vostre viscere, concepite moralmente. … La donna che sa educare, che plasma una intelligenza, che sviluppa un'anima, è madre anche se fanciulla; occupa quindi la prima dignità femminile" [Be mothers. If your body has not given birth in pain to the child of your entrails, conceive morally. ... The woman who knows how to educate, who moulds an intelligence, who develops a soul, is a mother, even if she is a child, and therefore occupies the first female dignity] (864). Suggesting to her readers the maternal instinct and role as the basis for women's redemption and empowerment within patriarchal society rather than the basis for female oppression that the maternal instinct and role had thus far represented, Neera confirms the need for the rediscovery and valorization of the maternal figure within patriarchal society.

Neera's Mothers: *L'amuleto, La vecchia casa, Il romanzo della fortuna and Duello d'anime*

The "new woman" outlined by Neera in her theoretical production and portrayed in the novels of her later years is a woman who valorizes her feminine qualities and comes to appreciate her self-worth, independently of men. The heroines of Neera's later production are no longer women whose only form of fulfillment is tied to becoming wives, as in her early novels. In her later production, Neera depicts the opportunity for female empowerment in the representation of women who find dignity, fulfillment and social redemption in their mission as mothers and educators. Neera suggests that women's natural ability to educate and nurture constitutes an essential aspect of their maternal mission. In the article "Tutte madri," she identifies educator as a role for which women are superior to men, exalting precisely the characteristics, such as readiness and shrewdness, presented by positivist thinkers as indicators of female inferiority: "Sì, più pronta, più astuta, più agile, la donna elevata e saggia si servirà anche di queste attitudini particolari per raggiungere i suoi fini educativi, quei fini che essa sola può far trionfare per la gloria eterna della verità" [Yes, more ready, more astute, more agile, the elevated and wise woman will also make use of these particular qualities to achieve her educational ends, those ends which she alone can make triumph for the eternal glory of truth] (*Le idee di una donna* 866). Neera proposes to her readers a new order that values women's contribution to society by encouraging women to recognize the nobility of their natural qualities. Her representation of women who devote themselves to a uniquely feminine goal represents her literary response to the *femme fatale* figure typical of much literature of the period. Neera's protagonists from the advanced phase of her literary production reject the male order that objectifies and humiliates women in favor of a female order, recognized and constructed by women, which privileges their innate maternal qualities.

In *L'amuleto* (1897), Myriam is initially portrayed as another daughter figure typical of Neera's early novels, women in need of the paternal figure's guidance in their search for fulfillment. Wife and mother in a loveless marriage, Myriam begins a relationship with a man that opens her eyes to spiritual and intellectual elevation. Their conversations make Myriam aware of a "mondo superiore" [superior world] and, spurred by his advice, she begins to read and reflect on what she reads. Her newfound belief in a superior kind of love, which includes a newly discovered dedication to her maternal duty, leads Myriam to reject his passionate declaration of love one day, although she questions whether he understands the reason for her refusal: "che solo da una ispirazione alta poteva nascere un amore come il mio?" [that only from a high inspiration could a love like mine be born?] (Neera, *L'amuleto* 500). In the same years, Neera dedicates attention also in her theoretical production to the ideal of platonic love, defining it in *Il libro di mio figlio* (1891) as the highest possible elevation of the senses between men and women: "l'amore vero, umano … che redima la donna dalla sua abbietta condizione sessuale; l'amore che freni i nobili e disperati tentativi di nichilismo; l'amore che infiammi di una religione nuova gl'increduli, che desti i pigri, che anima i codardi, che ispiri i generosi" [true, human love ... that redeems the woman from her abject sexual condition; love that curbs the noble and desperate attempts at nihilism; love that inflames the unbelievers with a new religion, that awakens the lazy, that animates the cowards, that inspires the generous] (717). Neera implements this ideal form of love and relationship between men and women in the novel *L'amuleto* through the character of Myriam, who exemplifies the ideal combination of moral behavior, maternal instinct and platonic love. Myriam is Neera's "new woman," a protagonist who no longer passively undergoes the oppression of the father figure, as the female characters of previous novels do, but liberates herself from the position of woman-child through the recognition of her superior role as woman and mother.

The female protagonist's role in *La vecchia casa* (1900) is initially determined by her desire to be the defender of her father's principles, considering herself to be the sole heir of his teachings on generosity and morality. Anna's desire to embrace her father's teachings prevents her from fulfilling her personal aspirations and sexuality, as the following passage reveals: "Anna non aveva pensato mai all'amore… Chi avrebbe dunque amato? Il ricordo di suo padre la occupava tanto che sembrava non dovesse restare nessun posto per altri"[Anna had never thought about love... Who would she love then? The memory of her father occupied her so much that it seemed there should be no place left for anyone else] (Neera, *La vecchia casa* 111). Anna associates spiritual purity, generosity and nobility with her father, while she links physical and sensual love to her mother, whom she discovers had an adulterous affair, and the sister she finds out was born from her mother's affair. Condemning her mother as a woman, for succumbing to an impure love, and as a daughter, for not upholding the example of honor and nobility represented by her father, Anna comes to identify completely with the father's example, considering herself the champion of his high standards of morality. Anna's rejection of the maternal figure in the first half of the novel also brings her to deny her attraction for Flavio because it represents the kind of physical love she associates with the mother's example. As the novel progresses, however, Anna's opinion of her mother evolves, similar to that experienced also by the female protagonist of Aleramo's *Una donna*, and she comes to appreciate and value the maternal model: "Una dolcezza somma la invase, la penetrò. Le parve che morbide braccia la cingessero cercandole il cuore con una tenerezza immateriale. Ricordava ella mai un abbraccio di sua madre? Così doveva essere l'abbraccio di una madre" [A sweet sensation invaded her, penetrated her. It seemed to her that soft arms surrounded her, looking for her heart with an immaterial tenderness. Did she ever remember a hug from her mother? This is what a mother's embrace must be like] (Neera, *La vecchia casa* 234–235). *La vecchia casa* presents another female figure who comes to realize and appreciate the value of the maternal figure and instinct, welcoming also her role as maternal guide and friend to Flavio. In forgiving her mother and sister, Anna breaks out of the oppressive paternal order "che spoglia la madre delle sue qualità" [that takes away the qualities of the mother] (Muraro 11), teaching women to reject the maternal model. *La vecchia casa* encourages women to value each other and overcome the barriers, set in place by patriarchal society, between women.

In *Il romanzo della fortuna* (1906), Neera again portrays the development of the female protagonist from woman-child, who negates her sexuality and desires for personal fulfillment, to woman-mother, who finds fulfillment in the maternal instinct. In the first half of the novel, Chiarina, fulfilling the role of the selfless female figure, subordinates her happiness and aspirations to those of others. When her brother Giovanni needs money to buy capital in the store he manages, Chiarina finances his economic endeavor with her inheritance, intended for her trousseau, rejecting the possibility of marriage so that she can fulfill what she considers to be her sisterly duty. Similar to other self-sacrificing sisters in Neera's production, such as Teresa, Chiarina devotes attention to her personal desires and aspirations only after serving others, repressing her desire for love and her sexuality to the point of becoming desexualized: "La signora Chiarina, per tutto il quartiere, non era una donna" [Ms. Chiarina, for the whole neighborhood, was not a woman] (Neera, *Il romanzo della fortuna* 190). As the novel progresses, however, Chiarina comes to find self-fulfillment in the maternal role and in the value of her instincts for nurturing others, as revealed through actions such as caring for two children who have been abandoned by their mother, tending to the members of the family that adopted her after the death of her parents and primarily through her understanding of her role as woman: "Materna nel suo profondo e retto istinto femminile, se al suo fianco non era riserbata la grazia di procreare, ella si sentiva madre per lo slancio ardente dell'affetto, per la intelligenza della comprensione, per la spontaneità della dedizione. Era così che intendeva la sua parte di donna" [Motherly in her deep and upright feminine instinct, if the grace to procreate was not reserved for her womb, she felt motherly for the ardent impulse of affection, for the intelligence of understanding, for the spontaneity of dedication. This is how she understood her role as a woman] (Neera, *Il romanzo della fortuna* 230). In the conclusion of the novel, Chiarina finds her place in society through the maternal role, achieving personal fulfillment rather than merely helping others obtain their aspirations.

The female protagonist of *Duello d'anime* (1911) comes to value her role as mother and recognize her self-worth independent of her relationship with men. Minna, whose social status as member of the working class accounts initially for her lack of self-esteem, falls in love with Filippo Consolo, a Dannunzian *superuomo* [superman] figure who does not recognize women as worthy life companions. Minna's low social status differentiates her from Neera's typical female protagonist, whose middle-class environment reflects the writer's own upbringing, providing an important example of this writer's attention to a range of social contexts. Minna's intense need to feel valued prevents her from realizing that Filippo views her exclusively as a sexual object, convinced of her innate inferiority. When she becomes pregnant with his child, he marries her only to avoid tarnishing his chances for a political career. Initially Minna views loving and serving Filippo as a way to elevate herself both socially and intellectually, repressing her desire for reciprocated love in the belief that she will one day earn Filippo's recognition and love. As the novel progresses, however, she comes to value her personal worth, no longer seeking fulfillment through her husband but in herself, through the elevation of her mind, and particularly through the recognition of her role as mother. Recognizing her "dignità di madre e di continuatrice" [dignity as mother and continuer] (Neera, *Duello d'anime* 607), Minna finds strength in the dignity of her mission. Neera contrasts Filippo's self-centered and unscrupulous nature and ambitions to Minna's altruistic ideal of self-elevation. In the conclusion of the novel, Filippo dies from illness, and Minna rejects the opportunity to remarry, feeling strong enough in her role as mother to continue on her own. Minna no longer pursues fulfillment in serving a man but in the maternal role and in advancing her own personal ideal of intellectual and moral ennoblement.

Christina Mazzoni notes in *Maternal Impressions: Pregnancy and Childbirth in Literature and Theory* (2002) that fin-de-siècle women writers' texts depicting the maternal are remarkable because they "both reproduce the stereotypes of womanhood and/as motherhood, begotten by patriarchal discourse, and conceive of alternative constructions" (36). Along the same lines, in "Maternal Prescriptions and Descriptions in Post-Unification Italy" (2013), Ursula Fanning notes regarding women writers' literary production depicting maternity: "They are anything but straightforward in their description of the maternal, but they refuse to allow patriarchy to have it all its own way. They do not allow the prescriptions around the maternal to 'own' maternal discourse; they present, instead, complex, not always positive, but always challenging alternatives. In many ways they are, like the experiences they describe, transformative." (31). The female figure proposed by Neera in her theoretical and later narrative production is strongly rooted in her time, forced to confront the restrictions of a society which relegates women to roles that are socially conceived and constructed as secondary, those of wife, mother, daughter or spinster. Yet Neera's "new woman" is also projected toward the future, indicating women a path that leads to liberation from society's restrictive and subordinated roles by illustrating the possibility for women to create a new role for themselves, one based on the recognition of their worth. Her creation of a literary space in which women can find dignity and strength is redeeming and empowering. It is also because of her work as writer that Neera manages to break out of that secondary role herself. Cixous confirms the importance of writing as a tool of empowerment for women: "It is by writing, from and toward women, and by taking up the challenge of speech which has been governed by the phallus, that women will confirm women in a place other than that which is reserved in and by the symbolic, that is, in a place other than silence" (881). Neera's later works succeed in breaking the daughter's silence by suggesting the possibility for female redemption and empowerment in the portrayal of an order that exalts, rather than denigrates, women's qualities.

Notes

1 Pierobon discusses the contradictory representations of the father figure in Neera's narrative. See Pierobon 42–49.

2 Neera's representation of hysteria reveals an understanding of the disease that reflects contemporary scientific thought regarding female hysteria as the physical manifestation of repressed sexuality. French physician Jean-Martin Charcot (1825–93), observing hysterical patients at the Salpetrière clinic in Paris in the years 1870–90, was the first to dedicate serious medical attention to female hysteria, defining the manifestations of hysteria as physical signs of a disease that derives from psychic trauma. See Charcot 133–161. Sigmund Freud, student of Charcot for a brief period at Salpetrière, studied the physical symptoms of hysteria as resulting from the repression of a traumatic experience. See Breuer and Freud, Showalter, *The Female Malady* 145–164 and King 3–90.

3 She understood her father's reasons: she had lived too much in that environment and in that alone, not to be persuaded that her condition as a woman imposed first of all resignation to her destiny - a destiny she was not free to direct - which she had to accept as it came to her, cut off from the needs of the family, subjected to the needs and desires of others.

4 From the very first time Lydia appeared in society, she immediately understood the important place that the skilled, cunning, unscrupulous, elegant and provocative woman holds. But in her eagerness to grasp this truth in order to profit from it, she overlooked one main observation: she did not take into account the immense gap that runs between the married woman and the spinster: everything that is allowed to the former, is forbidden to the latter. She believed that her ingenuity and wealth were enough to give her independence, believing herself to be strong enough to overcome secular prejudices.

5 We see women everywhere. You don't publish a book, a score, a program, that doesn't have a prosaic female figure on the cover, almost always naked. The shop windows are full of photographs of women. The luck of theaters rests on women. The most serious newspapers dedicate fashion chronicles to women and record the triumphs of professional beauties. Finally, every man has a matchbox in his pocket with two types of women, the blonde and the brunette; but in such abundance of women, the woman gets lost.

6 For honest women ... love can only be a duty or a sin; a contract entered into, signed, rendered sacrament, rendered civil duty, equal to the sacred order or the sale of a farm; or a split from convenience, law, religion, honor.

7 Time passed, and from anguished immobility Marta entered a state of sensual hallucination. With an unconscious hand she untied the hooks of her dress, loosened the ribbons, yielding to a mysterious sensation of abandonment, with skin-deep shivers, her mouth thirsty, dry, her arms desperately open. ... Lost in the images of love she would let her hair down, and twisting it around her face, she would breath in its youthful aroma, moaning her name - Marta, Marta! ...Time went by again, until the excitement left her exhausted, her limbs weak, her eyes battered and wavering.

8 See Nardi 89–92 for a discussion of the link in *L'indomani* between sensual love and maternal love.

9 Neera's articles on the *questione femminile,* originally published in journals such as *Vita Nuova, Il Marzocco* and *L'Idea Liberale,* were later collected for publication in the volumes *Battaglie per un'idea* and *Le idee di una donna.*

10 See numbers 16, 28 and 29 of the April 16, July 9 and July 16, 1893, issues of *L'Idea Liberale.*

11 Neera's articles published in response to Lombroso were later published in the 1898 volume *Battaglie per un'idea.* Citations will be taken from this text.

12 There, there, I know Mr. Lombroso's opinions on woman's alleged inferiority, but I am persuaded that he doesn't believe it either. How can a naturalist admit that, using the same means, one can bring into the world alternately superior and inferior beings? One might believe it, perhaps, if males made men.

13 It's too masculine to be sincere feminism. The efforts that are made to equalize men clearly show that women no longer recognize themselves in the integrity of their own value, and it is this value of theirs that I defend with outspoken ardor, dedicating my efforts to women who accept with simplicity and nobility their great mission, that is, making true feminism.

14 Formed differently physiologically, they have received from nature itself the task of different vital functions; and since no progress of civilization will make a man a mother, there is neither material nor moral reason for women to submit to the training of male occupations.
15 See Baldacci v–xii, Sanguineti 293–295 and Sanvitale v–xvi.
16 See Irigaray 11–21 and 92–101.
17 See Lonzi 11–61.

References

Amatangelo, Susan. *Figuring Women. A Thematic Study of Giovanni Verga's Female Characters.* Madison, Fairleigh Dickinson UP, 2004.

Arslan, Antonia and Anna Folli, editors. *Monastero e altri racconti.* Milan, Scheiwiller, 1987.

——— and Maria Grazia Raffaele, editors. *Fanfulla della domenica.* Treviso, Canova, 1981.

——— and Patrizia Zambon, editors. *Il sogno aristocratico. Angiolo Orvieto e Neera. Corrispondenza 1889–1917.* Milan, Guerini, 1990.

Azzolini, Paola. "*Lydia* o la tentazione della scrittura." *Ritratto di signora. Neera (Anna Radius Zuccari) e il suo tempo*, edited by Antonia Arslan and Marina Pasqui, Milano, Guerini, 1999, pp. 17–29.

Baldacci, Luigi. Introduction. *Teresa*, by Neera, Turin, Einaudi, 1976, pp. v–xii.

Breuer, Josef and Sigmund Freud. *L'Isteria*, translated by Celso Balducci, Rome, Newton, 1979.

Charcot, Jean Martin. *La Donna dell'isteria*, translated by Maria Grazia Amati, Milan, Spirali/Vel, 1989.

Cixous, Hélène. "The Laugh of the Medusa," translated by Keith Cohen and Paula Cohen. *Signs* vol. 1, no. 4, 1976, pp. 875–893.

Fanning, Ursula. "Maternal Prescriptions and Descriptions in Post-Unification Italy." *Women and Gender in Post-Unification Italy. Between Private and Public Spheres*, edited by Katharine Mitchell and Helena Sanson. Peter Lang, 2013, pp. 13–37.

Freud, Sigmund. *Dora. An Analysis of a Case of Hysteria*, translated by Philip Rieff, New York, Simon & Schuster, 1997.

Gilbert, Sandra and Susan Gubar. *The Madwoman in the Attic: The Woman Writer and the Nineteenth Century Literary Imagination.* New Haven: Yale UP, 1979.

Hosker, Lucy. "The Spinster in the Works of Neera and Matilde Serao: Other or Mother?" *Women and Gender in Post-Unification Italy. Between Private and Public Spheres*, edited by Katharine Mitchell and Helena Sanson, Peter Lang, 2013, pp. 67–91.

Irigaray, Luce. *Etica della differenza sessuale.* Milan, Feltrinelli, 1985.

King, Helen. "Once upon a Text. Hysteria from Hippocrates." *Hysteria before Freud*, edited by S. L. Gilman, Berkeley, U of California P, 1993, pp. 3–90.

Kroha, Lucienne. *The Woman Writer in Late 19th Century Italy: Gender and the Formation of Literary Identity*. Lewiston, Mellen, 1992.

Libreria delle Donne di Milano. *Non credere di avere dei diritti*. Turin, Rosenberg & Sellier, 1987.

Lonzi, Carla. *Sputiamo su Hegel. La donna clitoridea e la donna vaginale*. Milan, Rivolta femminile, 1974.

Mazzoni, Cristina. *Maternal Impressions: Pregnancy and Childbirth in Literature and Theory*. Ithaca, Cornell UP, 2002.

Mitchell, Katharine. "Neera's Refiguring of Hysteria as *Nervosismo* in *Teresa* and *L'Indomani*." *Rethinking Neera*, edited by Katharine Mitchell and Catherine Ramsey-Portolano. *The Italianist*, no. 30, 2010, pp. 101–122.

Morandini, Giuliana. *La voce che è in lei. Antologia della narrativa femminile italiana tra '800 e '900*. Milan, Bompiani, 1980.

Muraro, Luisa. *L'ordine simbolico della madre*. Roma, Riuniti, 1991.

Nardi, Isabella. "'Le cattive madri': Note sul tema della maternità nei romanzi dannunziani e oltre." *Maternità, trasgressività e letteratura*, edited by Ada Neiger, Naples, Liguori, 1993, pp. 79–97.

Neera. *Addio*! 1877. Milan, Baldini & Castoldi, 1919.

———. *Battaglie per un'idea*. 1898. Milan, Baldini & Castoldi, 1898.

———. *Duello d'anime*. 1911. *Neera*, edited by Benedetto Croce, Milan, Garzanti, 1942, pp. 501–654.

———. *Il castigo*. 1881. Turin, L. Roux, 1891.

———. *Il libro di mio figlio*. 1891. *Neera*, edited by Benedetto Croce, Milan, Garzanti, 1942, pp. 701–749.

———. *Il marito dell'amica*. 1885. Milan, Galli, 1891.

———. *Il romanzo della fortuna*. 1905. Milan, Antongini, 1906.

———. *L'amuleto*. 1897. *Neera*, edited by Benedetto Croce, Milan, Garzanti, 1942, pp. 419–500.

———. *L'indomani*. 1890. Palermo, Sellerio, 1990.

———. *La Regaldina*. 1883. Milan, Dumolard, 1884.

———. *La vecchia casa*. 1900. Milan, Treves, 1910.

———. *Le idee di una donna*. 1903. Neera, edited by Benedetto Croce, Milan, Garzanti, 1942, pp. 777–867.

———. *Lydia*. 1887. Neera, edited by Benedetto Croce, Milan, Garzanti, 1942, pp. 177–320.

———. *Teresa*, edited by Luigi Badacci, Turin, Einaudi, 1976.

Pierobon, Ermenegilda. "Neera e le implicazioni del mito del padre: simboli e metafore di personalità dissociata." *Canadian Journal of Italian Studies*, vol. 14, 1991, pp. 42–49.

Ramsey-Portolano, Catherine. "A Modern Feminist Reading of the Maternal Instinct in Neera." *Rethinking Neera*, edited by Katharine Mitchell and Catherine Ramsey-Portolano, *The Italianist*, vol. 30, 2010, pp. 50–68.

Sanguineti, Edoardo. "Madre due volte." *Giornalino secondo 1976–1977*. Turin, Einaudi, 1979, pp. 293–295.

Santovetti, Olivia. "Neera (1846–1918). The World Seen from the Window: Reading, Writing, and the Power of Fantasy." *The Italianist*, vol. 33, no. 3, Oct. 2012, pp. 388–402.

Sanvitale, Francesca, editor. *Invito alla lettura di Neera*. Florence, Vallecchi, 1977.

Showalter, Elaine. *A Literature of Their Own: British Women Novelists from Bronte to Lessing*. Princeton, Princeton UP, 1977.

——— *The Female Malady*. New York, Pantheon, 1985.

West, Rebecca. "Women in Italian." *Italian Studies in North America*, edited by Massimo Ciavolella and Amilcare A. Iannucci, Ottawa, Dovehouse, 1994, pp. 195–212.

Zambon, Patrizia. "La narrativa realista nei romanzi d'autrice di fine Ottocento." *Problemi*, vol. 108, 1997, pp. 166–177.

3 Neera the *Verist* Woman Writer

In this chapter, I will demonstrate Neera's rightful role, one that has been largely overlooked by critics throughout the years, within the Italian literary canon as *verist* writer by illustrating her active participation in and contribution to the movement.[1] I will analyze public and private documents in the form of literary reviews, book prefaces and epistolary correspondences to demonstrate Neera's declared interest in participating in the literary movement that swept through Italy in the years 1870–90 as well as the high regard expressed for her work by acclaimed *veristi*. Lastly, the examination of the *verist* qualities of *Teresa*, Neera's most acclaimed novel, will confirm her adherence to the stylistic and thematic characteristics of *verismo* and her rightful position within the Italian literary canon as *verista*.

Naturalism and *Verismo*

Verismo developed as a literary movement in late nineteenth-century Italy in the wake of French naturalism, thanks largely to the circulation in the Italian context of the works of writers such as Edmond and Jules de Goncourt, Émile Zola, Gustave Flaubert and Guy Maupassant, whom Luigi Capuana recognized as "i nostri predecessori, i nostri maestri stranieri" [our predecessors, our foreign teachers] (29) in his 1885 volume *Per l'arte* (For art), a fundamental text for the theoretical elaboration of the naturalist movement in Italy.[2] Capuana was strongly influenced by the literary production of Zola, the first writer to purposefully adopt the term *naturalisme* in reference to his literary program when he wrote in 1867 in the preface to the second edition of his novel *Thérèse Raquin* that "[l]e groupe d'ècrivains naturalistes auquel j'ai l'honneur d'appartenir a assez de courage ed d'activite pour produire des oeuvres fortes, portant en elles leur défense" [[t]he group of naturalist writers to which I have the honor to belong has enough courage and activity to produce strong works, putting forth their defense in them] (IX). The naturalist novel, as outlined by Zola in his 1880 essay *Le roman experimental* (The experimental novel), employs a "scientific" method of studying man, human nature and society through the objective portrayal of reality. In the following passage from *Le roman expérimental*, Zola reveals his faith in naturalist art's ability to reveal fundamental truths: "Nous montrons le mécanisme de l'utile e du nuisible, nous dégageons le déterminisme des phénomènes humains et sociaux, our qu'on puisse un jour dominer et diriger ces phénomènes" [We show the mechanism of the useful and the harmful, we show the determinism of human and social phenomena, so that we can one day dominate and direct these phenomena] (29). In the entry on *verismo* in *Encyclopedia of Italian Literary Studies* (2007), Gloria Lauri-Lucente defines the paradigmatic features of the French naturalist novel as:

> the rejection of the idealism of Romanticism; the dispassionate portrayal of moral and social deprivation or some aspect of hereditary pathology; the programmatic claim to 'impersonality' that involves the disappearance of the readily identifiable position of the narrator in relation to the characters being represented; and the denunciation of corrupt aspects of contemporary society. (1972)

The attention of Italian writers Capuana and Giovanni Verga to the tenets of French naturalism brought about the theoretical and artistic elaboration of the movement in the Italian context known as *verismo*. Capuana greeted Verga's short story *Nedda* (1874) as the beginning of a new narrative tradition in the Italian context: "Quando il Verga scrisse la *Nedda* forse non credeva di avere trovato un nuovo filone nella miniera quasi intatta del romanzo italiano" [When Verga wrote *Nedda* perhaps he did not believe he had found a new seam in the almost intact mine of the Italian novel] (*Studii sulla letteratura contemporanea* 80). In the letter to Salvatore Farina that opens the short story *L'amante di Gramigna* (Gramigna's lover, 1880), which can be considered a manifesto for *verismo*, Verga refers to his short story as "un documento umano" [a human document] (*Le novelle* 213) and outlines similar objectives to those expressed above by Zola:

> Il misterioso processo per cui le passioni si annodano, si intrecciano, maturano, si svolgono nel loro cammino sotterraneo, nei loro andirivieni che spesso sembrano contradditori, costituirà

> per lungo tempo ancora la possente attrattiva di quel fenomeno psicologico che forma l'argomento di un racconto, e che l'analisi moderna si studia di seguire con scrupolo scientifico. (*Le novelle* 213)[3]

To achieve such objectives, Verga privileges the doctrine of the impersonality of art, identifying in the above-mentioned letter his literary goal of producing a work that "sembrerà essersi fatto da sé, avere maturato ed esser sorto spontaneo come un fatto naturale, senza serbare alcun punto di contatto col suo autore" [will seem to have made itself, to have matured and emerged spontaneously as a natural fact, without retaining any point of contact with its author] (*Le novelle* 213). Italian *veristi* restrict narratorial description to a minimum, adopting instead stylistic characteristics such as dialogue, interior monologue and free indirect speech which allow the characters to come to life in the immediacy of their passions and sufferings with limited narratorial intervention. Unlike French naturalism, Italian *verismo* is characterized by a strong interest in the portrayal of regional realities, as Giulio Ferroni notes in *Storia della letteratura italiana. Dall'Ottocento al Novecento* (History of Italian literature. From 1800 to 1900, 1991): "Dal confronto con il naturalismo francese e dall'interesse per le realtà regionali derivano i maggiori risultati del verismo italiano" [From the comparison with French naturalism and the interest for regional realities derive the major results of Italian realism] (406). The portrayal of nineteenth-century rural Sicily, in the works of Sicilian writers Verga, Capuana and Federico De Roberto, is traditionally cast as constituting the essence of *verismo*. In *Storia della letteratura italiana. Dall'Ottocento al Novecento* (History of Italian literature. From 1800 to 1900, 1968), Giulio Cattaneo recognizes other factors, in addition to regionalism and the impersonal art form, as defining characteristics of *verismo*, allowing for the inclusion within the *verist* realm of additional writers whose work includes a focus on other regional realities, social classes and stylistic elements:

> Al cosiddetto verismo appartiene in senso più esteso quella narrativa che ha puntato sul 'documento umano' sviluppando con intenti scientifici la rivoluzione romantica. Il 'documento umano' poteva essere estratto da qualsiasi ambiente (aristocratico, borghese, popolano) come è dimostrato dal progetto del ciclo dei 'Vinti' ideato dal Verga, dalle opere del Capuana e

> del De Roberto, dal *Paese di Cuccagna* della Serao dove personaggi di tutte le classi sociali sono passati ugualmente in rassegna. (332)[4]

The representation of regional contexts other than that of Sicily and of middle- and upper-class contexts in the works of authors such as Serao, Mario Pratesi and Renato Fucini, for example, demonstrates that the movement was not limited to the portrayal of a specific geographic context, social realm or even specific stylistic techniques. Cattaneo refers to Serao's "verismo sentimentale" [sentimental realism] (375) in her portrayal of the Neapolitan proletariat as well as bourgeois and upper classes in works such as *Il ventre di Napoli* (The underbelly of Naples, 1884), *Virtù di Checchina* (Checchina's virtue, 1884) and *Il paese di Cuccagna* (Cuccagna town, 1891), while classifying Pratesi and Fucini as *veristi* for their depiction of Tuscany's peasant classes in works such as Pratesi's *L'eredità* (The legacy, 1889) and Fucini's *Le veglie di Neri* (The Vigils of Neri, 1883). Such considerations on *verismo* justify examination of the work of Milanese writer Neera, whose portrayal of the Lombard bourgeois female reality demonstrates a scientific approach to examining the "human document" privileged by naturalist and *verist* writers of her time.

Neera and the *Veristi:* Public and Private Exchanges on *Verismo*

Capuana first takes notice of Neera as a *verist* writer with a review of her collection of short stories *Novelle gaie* (Gay tales, 1879) and her novel *Un nido* (A nest, 1880), praising her "imaginazione vivace" [vivacious imagination] and "ingegno non ordinario" [unusual wit] (*Studii sulla letteratura contemporanea* 88). Although Capuana criticizes the "mondo un po' artifiziale" [slightly artificial world] (*Studii sulla letteratura contemporanea* 91) represented in *Un nido,* he notes that the novel nonetheless demonstrates the essential characteristics of the new art form promoted by the critic in those years. Capuana observes certain traits in Neera's most recent production, such as "un notevole vigore di rappresentazione, una certa sottigliezza nell'osservare" [a notable vigor in representation, a certain subtleness in observation] (*Studii sulla letteratura contemporanea* 91), that reveal her potential for participating in *verismo.* In the same year, a review of *Un nido* by literary critic Federigo Verdinois praises the novel's "realismo alla Zola"[5]

[Zola-esque realism], confirming Neera as part of a group of writers influenced by and participating in the literary movement of French naturalist inspiration.

Two additional public documents, Capuana's dedication to Neera of the 1888 edition of his novel *Homo* (Man) and the third edition of *Giacinta* (1889), further confirm Neera's status as *verist* writer in those years. The *Homo* dedication, entitled "Come io divenni novelliere" [How I became a novelist] and subtitled "Confessione a Neera," [Confession to Neera] is significant as "la testimonianza più ricca, viva e utile sulla propria evoluzione culturale lasciataci dall'autore" [the richest, most fresh and useful testimony on his cultural evolution left us by the author], (Madrignani 238). The choice of confession as subtitle becomes apparent in Capuana's lighthearted reference to the demon of novels and short stories that took possession of him, causing him to be blinded "dal torbido fumo balzacchiano, flaubertiano, zoliano, degoncourtiano, il peggio fumo che mai ingombrasse il limpido cielo dell'arte, e che mai lo appestasse colle sue fetide esalazioni!" [by the murky Balzacian, Flaubertian, Zolian, Degoncourtian smoke, the worst smoke that ever cluttered the limpid sky of art, and that ever contaminated it with its stinking fumes ("Come io divenni novelliere" xxix). In *Studi sulla letteratura contemporanea* (Studies on contemporary literature), Capuana acknowledges, in fact, certain concerns regarding the new art form proposed by *verismo*, recognizing, however, the necessity of artistic innovation: "È innegabile che la severità quasi scientifica dell'arte moderna opprime, stanca, fa male al cuore. Ma dall'altro lato è anch'innegabile che l'arte dove non sia passato il soffio del pensiero moderno non è più un'arte vitale e che abbia valore" [It is undeniable that the almost scientific severity of modern art oppresses, wears out, hurts the heart. But on the other hand it is also undeniable that art, where the breath of modern thought has not passed, is no longer a vital and valuable art] (*Studii sulla letteratura contemporanea* 91). Capuana's motivation for dedicating his confessions to Neera can be understood from the following passage:

> Ho fatto bene sceglìendovi a mia confessora? Siete Voi così libera da ogni terreno vincolo da poter fungere da giudice imparziale secondo le più pure dottrine della chiesa letteraria? Ahimè, avete artisticamente peccato e continuate, ahimè, a peccare anche voi, per quanto la vostra felice condizione di donna vel consente! Anche voi, ahimè, vi siete, a poco a poco, lasciata adescare dalla eresia, spero inconscientemente: e sarà la vostra difesa innanzi a Dio! ("Come io divenni novelliere" xxxiii–iv)[6]

The references to Capuana and Neera's shared actions and responsibilities, expressed through the metaphor of literary sins, reveal, however jokingly, Capuana's consideration of Neera as a writer dedicated like himself to the "heresy" of literary innovation, a sin that she had not only committed previously but continued to commit in 1888, a reference to the recent publication of novels such as *Teresa* and *Lydia*.

In the preface to the third edition of *Giacinta*, published in 1889 and entitled simply "A Neera" [To Neera], Capuana picks up *medias res* his thoughts on the evolution of the modern Italian novel from where he left off in *Homo*'s dedication. It is important to note in this context that Capuana dedicated the first edition of *Giacinta* in 1879 to Zola. Capuana's dedication of the novel's third edition to Neera, which aligns her with the principal representative of French naturalism and therefore the literary "father" of *verismo*, indicates his consideration of Neera as *verist* writer. In the conclusion of *Giacinta*'s 1889 preface, Capuana again refers to Neera as his accomplice in art: "E questo vi dimostri che forse soltanto noi, benché innanzi con gli anni e con tanta triste esperienza della vita, soltanto noi, in mezzo alla nuova generazione precocemente nauseata d'ideali, serbiamo ancora fede, a dispetto di tutto, alla infeconda illusione che è l'arte letteraria in Italia!" [And this proves to you that perhaps only we, despite the years and with so much sad experience of life, only we, in the midst of the new generation prematurely nauseated by ideals, still retain faith, in spite of everything, in the infectious illusion that is the literary art in Italy!] ("A Neera" 38). Capuana's reference to *noi* [us] must be interpreted as a reference exclusively to himself and Neera, representatives of a generation of writers that found themselves being pushed out of the literary scene by a newer, younger generation.

Neera responds in 1891 by dedicating to Capuana her *Confessioni letterarie*, in which she narrates the people and events that influenced the development of her artistic personality and literary vocation. She declares her intention to offer Capuana, whom she defines a "studios[o] di psicologia," [scholar of psychology] a human document, referencing a direct quote from Verga's introduction to *L'amante di Gramigna*.[7] Neera defines herself also a "scrittrice psicologica" [psychological writer] (*Confessioni letterarie* 894), thereby including herself within the same select group of writers. Neera's literary confessions were published as preface to the second edition of her novel *Il castigo*, which she describes as "il passo decisivo verso lo studio dal vero" [the decisive step towards learning from life] (*Confessioni letterarie* 872). *Il castigo*, published the year after *Un nido*, which Capuana praised but also criticized for its lack of realism, reflects Neera's decision to follow the critic's advice and dedicate herself entirely to the study of reality. It is possible to interpret, therefore, Neera's remark regarding *Il castigo* as her conscious decision in 1881, the year which also witnessed the publication of Verga's *verist* masterpiece *I Malavoglia*, to adhere to the *verist* doctrine of observing and faithfully representing reality. *Il castigo* marks Neera's first step, in fact, toward the analysis of the social and environmental conditions that lead to women's unhappiness. Neera demonstrates a *verist* understanding of art in the following description in *Confessioni letterarie* of the novel's protagonist: "Laura, nel *Castigo*, è un tipo umano. In lei vivono e si riassumono i palpiti di mille donne. Sicuro, non è simpatica, ma passò quel tempo in cui le eroine di un romanzo dovevano essere simpatiche ad ogni costo. Ella è meno e più che simpatica. È infelice" [Laura, in *Castigo*, is a human type. In her live and abound the palpitations of a thousand women. Sure, she's not nice, but there was a time when the heroines of a novel had to be nice at all costs. She's less and more than nice. She's unhappy] (873). Neera is not concerned with respecting morality or adhering to literary stereotypes of women, rather in her production of those years she strives to represent authentic female realities, such as that of the *zitella* or the hysteric. In *Italian Women Writers: Gender and Everyday Life in Fiction and Journalism,* Katharine Mitchell argues that *verist* poetics, which feature "the realistic and objective description of specific settings and individual situations" (13), afforded women writers an accepted means for exposing oppressive situations experienced by women at the time:

> Realist fiction purports to describe the "extratextual" world in an apparently faithful way, and in this respect we might think of it in similar terms to reportage. Regardless of whether non-fiction succeeds in representing reality, its professed referent is the extratextual world, which sharply distinguishes it from those pieces of writing that declare themselves fiction. (13)

The public exchange of ideas between Neera and Capuana regarding the current state of the Italian novel demonstrates Neera's active role in literary debates of the period, framing her as a point of reference for discussions on *verismo*. The consideration of private documents, in the form of letters exchanged between Neera and *verist* writers such as Capuana, Verga and Federico De Roberto, further contributes to an understanding of Neera's participation in *verismo*.[8] Such documents reveal a network of communication between writers who shared common ideas regarding the need for innovation of the Italian novel in those years, demonstrating the literary *fratellanza* [brotherhood] that existed between Neera and other *veristi* and their exchange of ideas on *verismo*.

Capuana and Neera's epistolary exchange reveals a relationship based on friendship and mutual respect between two writers who shared, in those years, a common understanding of art.[9] Although the beginning of the epistolary exchange dates to 1881, the two had already met in Countess Maffei's literary salon, and upon Capuana's return to Sicily in 1880, his correspondence with Neera began. Neera acknowledges Capuana as her instructor and seeks his approval throughout their exchange in the form of reviews of her work. Capuana's comments on Neera's novels throughout their epistolary exchange reveal his appreciation for her gradual progression and evolution as *verist* writer. On July 28, 1881, Capuana writes: "*Castigo* mantiene in gran parte le promesse del *Nido*, cosa che non accade di tutti i lavori e a tutti gli autori; anzi!" [*Castigo* largely keeps the promises of *Nido*, which is not the case with all works and with all authors; on the contrary!] (Arslan, "Luigi Capuana e Neera" 166). In a letter dated July 26, 1884, Capuana discusses Neera's latest novel *La Regaldina*, praising her "ingegno fino" [fine wit] and "le linee così maestralmente tracciate" [the lines so masterfully drawn] in order to note again the progress of Neera's literary style: "un grandissimo progresso nella padronanza della forma" [a great progress in the mastery of form] (Arlsan, "Luigi Capuana e Neera" 174). In this private epistolary review, Capuana compares Neera's female protagonist to that of Zola's latest novel *La joie de vivre* (The joy of living,1884): "La vostra Daria è più umana e più schiettamente donna della Paolina dell'ultimo romanzo dello Zola, colla quale ha qualche rassomiglianza" [Your Daria is more human and more outspokenly feminine than the Pauline of Zola's latest novel, with whom she has some resemblance] (Arslan, "Luigi Capuana e Neera" 174). In making Zola a point of reference for Neera's novel, one which Neera had surpassed according to the critic, Capuana reveals his high esteem of Neera as a writer capable of representing *il vero* [the real]. In a letter dated July 15, 1885, Capuana refers to Neera's latest novel *Il marito dell'amica* as "efficacissimamente vero" [extremely real] (Arslan, "Luigi Capuana e Neera" 185) and praises her ability to represent characters taken from life, when he writes: "Maria è stupendamente studiata" [Maria is beautifully studied] (Arslan, "Luigi Capuana e Neera" 185). Capuana reveals his awareness that Neera, as woman writer, is perhaps better able to represent the female reality: "Ah! Come diavolo dobbiamo fare noialtri scrittori maschili, se gli scrittori femminili ci tolgono il mestiere di mano e fanno assai meglio di noi?" [Ah! What the hell are we male writers supposed to do when female writers take our jobs away from us and do much better than we do?] (Arslan, "Luigi Capuana e Neera" 185). Acknowledging that Neera has progressed from her initial position of *scolara* [student] to almost surpassing her *maestro* [teacher], Capuana admits the competition that women writers represented for fin-de-siècle male writers. Given that much of Capuana's narrative of those years is dedicated to the study of female psychology, with works such as *Giacinta*, *Ribrezzo* (Repugnance, 1885) and *Profumo* (Profume, 1892), it is possible that throughout the course of their relationship, Capuana came to view Neera more as competitor than student, acquiring, as discussed earlier in this study, the attitude of many male writers and critics toward women writers.

The exchange between Neera and Verga also contributes to positioning Neera within a recognized group of *veristi.* The majority of the letters the two writers exchanged, 19 in all, date from 1884, a central year for the discussion on *verismo* in Italian literary circles. His letters reveal his "grande stima" [great esteem] (Arslan and Verdirame, "Giovanni Verga e Neera: un carteggio" 32) and "sincera ammirazione" [sincere admiration] (Arslan and Verdirame, "Giovanni Verga e Neera: un carteggio" 42)[10] for Neera's work. In a letter dated February 13, 1884, Verga declares the bond of literary brotherhood that unites him and Neera by addressing her as "caro confratello" [dear brother] (Arslan and Verdirame, "Giovanni Verga e Neera: un carteggio" 31). Verga establishes Neera as a member of a literary family, to which he also belongs, that could be none other than that of *verismo.*

Verga's use of the masculine form *confratello* reflects his esteem of Neera as writer and, at the same time, his reservations regarding women writers' literary talents. Verga's association of literary talent with masculine qualities, not unusual for the time as previously noted, is confirmed in another letter to Neera dated June 9, 1884: "Gentilissima Signora, e stavo per dire confratello, tanto Ella ha delle qualità virili nella nostra arte difficile, in cui tanti rinomatissimi portano la gonnella" [Dear Madam, and I was going to say brother, you have such virile qualities in our difficult art, in which so many famous people wear skirts] (Arslan and Verdirame, "Giovanni Verga e Neera: un carteggio" 36). With his reference to *nostra arte difficile*, Verga recognizes Neera's success in the profession practiced by both writers. In the same letter, Verga continues his praise of Neera's production and literary ability by recognizing, as Capuana had also done, the success she had already obtained as well as her future potential: "mi tratti da suo confratello nè grande nè piccolo, ma ammiratore sincero di quel che fa, ma più ancora di quel che può fare" [treat me as your brother, neither big nor small, but a sincere admirer of what you do, but even more of what you can do] (Arslan and Verdirame, "Giovanni Verga e Neera: un carteggio" 36).

Neera's correspondence with another *verista* of the period, Federico De Roberto, further confirms the extent of Neera's contacts with the most representative names of *verismo*.[11] The epistolary exchange spans from 1888, the year of De Roberto's review of Neera's *Lydia*,[12] to 1890 and consists of 18 letters. Beginning with Neera's letter to De Roberto thanking him for the favorable review of her novel, the *carteggio* [correspondence] reveals the writers' exchange of ideas on the art form in vogue in Italy in those years. In her first letter, Neera writes, "Ella non può forse immaginare che delicato piacere sia, per uno scrittore conosciuto, il trovare un lettore e un critico all'altezza dei concetti artistici che lo ispirano e questo non succede spesso!" [You cannot possibly imagine what a delicate pleasure it is, for a well-known writer, to find a reader and a critic up to the artistic concepts that inspire him and this does not often happen] (Arslan and Verdirame, "Neera a De Roberto" 251–252). Neera recognizes in De Roberto a reader and critic who, as member of Neera's same literary circle, is able to understand and appreciate the artistic concepts behind her work. In another letter, dated January 1, 1890, Neera alludes to belonging to the same literary family as De Roberto:

> Ha sentito il trionfo di Rovetta in *Barbarò*?[13] È un trionfo in famiglia, del quale dobbiamo essere lieti tutti per l'amore che ci lega nel gran nome dell'arte. (Arslan and Verdirame, "Neera a De Roberto" 257)[14]

Neera's public and private exchanges with the leading figures of *verismo* point to her active participation within the literary movement.

Teresa, a Verist Novel

The most direct testimony of the *verist* dimension of Neera's literary production derives from the analysis of her novel *Teresa*, her eighth novel, following works that had achieved a certain level of success with critics and public alike, such as *Un nido, La Regaldina* and *Il marito dell'amica.* In *Una giovinezza del secolo XIX,* Neera acknowledges, however, that the novel's critical success increased her recognition as writer: "devo confessare che solamente in seguito alla pubblicazione di *Teresa* si incominciò a prendermi sul serio" [I must confess that it wasn't until after the publication of *Teresa* that they began to take me seriously"(124).[15]

In *Teresa,* Neera represents the drama of the *zitella*, the unmarried woman whose fate in society is determined by societal customs and roles for women.[16] Neera finds the source of her representation in the observation of reality, one of the essential prerequisites of *verismo.* In *Una giovinezza del secolo XIX,* Neera reveals the novel's real-life inspiration:

> Tante fanciulle posarano inconsapevoli per la mia *Teresa*, ed una che si chiamava veramente Teresa mi bastò vederla una volta sola. Pallida e mesta, seduta in disparte dalle sue sorelle, che giovani ed allegre scherzavano tra loro, cuciva una camicia per il fidanzato lontano, fidanzato già da dieci anni, il quale non veniva mai, ed al quale ella pensava sempre. Queste due antitesi, l'indifferenza di lui, la costanza di lei: ecco il romanzo sorto in un attimo intero e vitale. (124)[17]

As Capuana argues in *Per l'arte*, it is the *verist* writer's responsibility not only to observe but also to interpret reality. In the simple observation of a young girl sewing a shirt, Neera imagines the context for her novel. In speaking of *Teresa*'s special significance for its female public, Neera further reveals in *Una giovinezza del secolo XIX*: "Era il dramma di tante anime femminili … e che avessi colpito nel segno me lo dissero innumerevoli lettere di ignote, e la loro commozione e le loro lagrime e il melanconico e pur dolce conforto di sentirsi comprese" [It was the drama of so many female souls ... and the countless letters I received from strangers told me that I had hit the mark, as well as their emotion and their tears and the melancholy and yet sweet comfort of feeling understood] (124). In *Teresa,* Neera gives voice to a multitude of women who suffer their condition in silence, without the means to effectively express their dissatisfaction or rebellion. Neera's observation and faithful representation of female reality in *Teresa* reflects her adherence to *verist* artistic principles in this phase of her literary career.

Neera's ability to allow her characters to speak for themselves is a central aspect of the *verist* nature of *Teresa*. The author's narrative distance is evident from the novel's opening scene, which describes the flooding of the Po River in the town of the novel's protagonist. The first lines of the novel, which present the scene void of any introductory element, immediately establish the style of narration-action in progress, characteristic of *verist* novels: "Coraggio, figliuoli, coraggio. Ne abbiamo, Signor Sindaco, ma la faccenda è brutta assai; temo che l'abbia da andar male per tutti" [Courage, young men, courage. We have it, Mr. Mayor, but it's a very bad thing; I'm afraid it's bad for everyone] (Neera, *Teresa* 3). Neera immerses the reader, ignorant of the name of the town, the type of event and the identity of the *figliuoli*, into the midst of the action and into the reality of her protagonists. Verga uses a similar technique in the opening scene of *I Malavoglia* in the presentation of people and places that have no significance for the reader who is not a member of the community represented in the novel. In a letter to Capuana, dated February 25, 1881, Verga explains the significance of such a technique:

> la confusione che dovevano produrvi in mente alle prime pagine tutti quei personaggi messivi faccia a faccia senza nessuna presentazione, come li aveste conosciuti sempre, e foste nato e vissuto in mezzo a loro, doveva scomparire mano mano col progredire della lettura, a misura che essi vi tornavano davanti, e vi si affermavano con nuove azioni ma senza messa in scena, semplicemente, naturalmente, era artificio voluto e cercato anch'esso, per evitare, perdonami il bisticcio, ogni artificio letterario, per darvi l'illusione completa della realtà. (*Lettere a Luigi Capuana* 162)[18]

Neera again avoids the use of *mise-en-scene* in passing directly from the scene of the catastrophe of the flooded river to the protagonist's home, where that night Teresa's mother is giving birth to her fifth child. Neera introduces the novel's protagonist through the mother's remark to her midwife: "Saranno quindici anni appunto il mese venturo" [It will be 15 years next month] (*Teresa* 14), referring to Teresa's birth 15 years earlier. The negativity of Teresa's condition as a woman is immediately presented in the mother's wish for her unborn child to be a boy and in her consideration that "le ragazze, poverette, che cos'hanno di buono a questo mondo?" [girls, poor things, what do they have that's good in this world?] (Neera, *Teresa* 14). Before Teresa is even named in the novel, her mother's words outline her role in society as a woman condemned to hope for little from life. Significantly, it is Teresa's mother, a woman already familiar with the possibilities for fulfillment that turn-of-the-century Italian society offers women, who reveals the female character's limited options. Neera allows the characters of the novel, the members of the social realm being portrayed, to speak for themselves and relay to the reader the circumstances being represented, thereby presenting a reality that seemed, as Verga suggests in *L'amante di Gramigna*, "essersi fatto da sé" [made by itself] (*Le novelle* 213).

Guido Baldi observes that Verga employs in his *verist* production the technique of "artificio della regressione" [artifice of regression] (46) to achieve the impersonal art form through the use of an anonymous narrator, whose point of view reflects that of the members of the society represented. Neera makes use of the same narrative technique to present the late nineteenth-century female reality, as in the following presentation of Teresa's aunt:

> La zia Rosa, nella placidezza serena di una vita di pianta, conservava un po' della bellezza statuaria che l'aveva gettata a diciotto anni nelle braccia di un uomo – senza che né l'uno né l'altra si amassero, perché lui aveva bisogno di trovar moglie per accudire al negozio; e lei era una ragazza da marito. (*Teresa* 39)[19]

Neera presents, from the perspective of a member of Teresa's community, the practical motivations which govern women's destiny as wife and caretaker. Furthermore, the final part of the above passage is an example of another stylistic technique utilized often by *veristi*, especially Verga, that of free indirect speech. By mingling the narrator's voice, expressed in the first part of the passage, with that of the character, Neera succeeds in adopting a stylistic technique that allows the characters to narrate themselves.

The novel follows Teresa's development from a young adolescent, innocent to the ways of the world and love, to a woman in the prime of her years who yearns for love, to a middle-aged woman who has seen her aspirations for love disappear. At age 15, Teresa first becomes aware of her body and questions whether she is attractive or not:

> Come erano bianche le sue braccia! Ella non aveva mai avuto tempo di guardarle, e le apparivano ora come le braccia di un'altra persona, così sottili, rotonde e bianche. Proprio non sapeva capacitarsi come fossero bianche, mentre il colorito del volto tendeva al bruno, ed anche il collo era bruno; solo scendendo sotto la clavicola, dove principiava il petto, il bianco riappariva. Questa ineguaglianza della sua pelle la sorprese; certo non doveva essere cosa normale. Allora, improvvisamente, fu assalita da un pensiero strano. Era essa bella o brutta? (Neera, *Teresa* 48)[20]

Through the portrayal of Teresa's sudden awareness of the difference between the color of her arms and that of her face and neck, exposed to the rays of the sun when she leaves the confines of her home, Neera reveals Teresa's role as the oldest daughter who does not have time to think of her own beauty and physicality. Teresa's interior monologue, another stylistic technique utilized often in *verist* production, reveals not only her naiveté regarding societal standards of beauty but also the conditions of her life so far which have not allowed the young protagonist time for any activity other than helping others. Later in the novel, Neera presents Teresa at the age of 19, now acutely aware of her limited prospects for finding a husband due to the economic limitations within her family, as the following exchange between the novel's protagonist and a friend reveals:

> E Teresina intanto pensava che dacché avevano mandato Carlino a Parma, per via del liceo, e tutti i mesi bisognava pagare la pensione, si parlava molto d'economia in casa sua – e non avevano più la donna di servizio – ed erano tre mesi ch'ella aspettava un paio di stivaletti nuovi. (*Teresa* 69)[21]

Teresa's thoughts, expressed in another example of Neera's use of free indirect speech, reveal her awareness of her fate as daughter, whose happiness and needs come second to those of the family's only male child, a fact that no one has to explain to her. Regardless of her naiveté, Teresa understands all too well the economic mechanisms that determine her fate within the family. When, three years later, her fiancé Orlandi asks permission to marry her, Teresa's father explains without hesitation the reason for his refusal to provide the "piccola somma per l'avviamento" [small sum to get started with] requested: "Mia figlia non ha dote. Ho quattro ragazze, signore, e se dovessi dare una dote a tutte quattro, non resterebbe altra risorsa a mio figlio che quella di andare a fare il contadino" [My daughter has no dowry. I have four girls, sir, and if I were to give a dowry to all four of them, my son would have no other outcome but to go and be a farmer] (Neera, *Teresa* 134). With the family's interests focused on the son's future success, Teresa must confront the reality that economic factors deny her the right to the future she desires.

Neera's stark portrayal, without embellishments of any kind, of Teresa's limited options constitutes, according to Luigi Baldacci, the essence of the novel's *verismo* due to "l'assenza di ogni ideale: nella misura stessa in cui alla protagonista è negata non solo la consolazione celeste, ma quella terrena del matrimonio e della maternità" [the absence of any ideal: to the very extent that the protagonist is denied not only heavenly consolation, but the earthly consolation of marriage and motherhood] (ix). Neera's attention to portraying the limited reality faced by women of her time and the social critique that emerges from such a portrayal recall similar observations of Verga's *verist* production. In *Questioni verghiane* (Vergian questions, 1969), Francesco Nicolosi refers to Verga's attention to representing "il senso del fato invincibile" [the sense of invincible fate] (35) that weighs upon the characters of his *verist* short stories and novels, whom Nicolosi describes as "poveri che siedono sul più basso gradino della scala sociale" [poor people sitting on the lowest rung of the social ladder] (35), members of a world "dominato dalle dure leggi economiche" [dominated by harsh economic laws] (Nicolosi 40). While there are clearly differences between the contexts and the social groups portrayed by Verga, that of the Sicilian peasants and fishermen, and the women of provincial Lombardy's middle-class represented by Neera, similarities exist in the depiction of society's "weak" who fight against a destiny dictated by forces beyond their control.

As noted earlier, *Teresa*, *Lydia* and *L'indomani* form a trilogy dedicated to the exploration of post-Unification Italian reality "dalla parte di lei" [from her side] (Arslan, *Dame, galline e regine* 128). In *Dame, galline e regine. La scrittura femminile italiana fra '800 e '900* (Ladies, hens and queens. Italian women's writing between 1800 and 1900, 1998), Arslan describes Neera's objective in these three novels: "disegnare con verosimiglianza caratteri di giovani donne poste di fronte alle varie occorrenze di un tipico destino femminile: lo zitellaggio, la caduta, il matrimonio" [to depict with verisimilitude characters of young women placed in front of the various occurrences of a typical female destiny: spinsterhood, disgrace, marriage, etc.] (128). Neera's trilogy can be considered in the context of naturalist and *verist* literary cycles of the period, such as Zola's *Rougon Macquart* novels, Honoré de Balzac's *La Comédie humaine* novels and short stories and Verga's programmed cycle of novels dedicated to *i vinti* [the defeated], outlined in the preface to *I Malavoglia.*[22] In *Confessioni letterarie,* Neera recognizes French naturalist novels as a point of reference for her work, especially the novels by Edmond and Jules de Goncourt focused on women:

> La donna, per lo scrittore analitico e sentimentale, è il soggetto di predilezione, la fonte inesauribile di simpatia e d'arte. Per citare solamente i fratelli Goncourt, essi hanno sette romanzi che portano un titolo di donna, che si imperniano sulla donna e si diramano per tutti i meandri più sottili e più complicati delle sensazioni femminili. (894)[23]

In "Cosa scrivevano le donne di fine Ottocento? (What did turn-of-the-century women write?, 1893)," Silvia Valisa refers to Neera's trilogy as "la più importante serie di romanzi sulle donne pubblicata intorno agli anni '80 dell'Ottocento" [the most important series of novels about women published in the years of the 1880s] (243). In the context of naturalist/*verist* works dedicated to the analysis of women's lives, it is important to consider also Capuana's works dedicated to examining the female condition: *Giacinta*, *Ribrezzo* and *Profumo*. Neera sheds further light on her literary project and goals of those years in the article "Le donne che piangono" (Women that cry) published in 1888 in *Fanfulla della domenica*, in which she defines herself a "*sperimentale o psichica*" [experimental or psychic] writer – two adjectives laden with literary references for the time – and affirms the need to denounce female suffering in society:

> Noi rechiamo alla luce del sole i derelitti e gli sventurati presentandoli alla vostra pietà. … La causa che meglio abbisogna di quest'opera paziente è la causa della donna. … Mi si disse ingiusta, pessimista, partigiana del mio sesso, quando in lavori scritti col più ardente amore del prossimo osai difendere la donna, la donna pura, la donna caduta, quella che ama e quella

> che non ama, la donna sempre, per ciò che è donna, vale a dire oppressa.[24]

With the reference to *noi*, Neera aligns herself with a group of writers whose objective was that of bringing to light oppressed existential and social realities.

Neera's Post-*Verismo* Production: Symbolism and Benedetto Croce

Although Neera was an active participant in the *verismo* movement in the 1880s, as demonstrated through reviews of her production of those years, public and private testimonials to her status as *verist* writer and an analysis of *Teresa*, she later turned her back on *verist* principles in favor of a new literary movement: symbolism. Neera's epistolary writings are an important source of information for an understanding of the evolution of her literary style, as her comments in a letter from 1893 to journalist Angiolo Orvieto reveal:

> Per parlare solamente della mia personalità letteraria osservo con meraviglia che quasi tutti i miei contemporanei si sono seduti o addormentati e molti fossilizzati sulla prima forma del loro ideale. Io ho già compiuto da un pezzo due evoluzioni ed ho incominciata la terza nella quale mi slancio con un ardore ed una freschezza che formano, per il momento, la mia maggiore felicità. (Arslan and Zambon 78–79)[25]

Neera reveals the search for innovation, "frutto di un continuo desiderio di miglioramento" [product of a continuous desire for improvement] (Arslan and Zambon 168), as one of the characteristics of her literary style. The exasperated representation of reality that characterizes Neera's early production reveals late romantic influences, acknowledged by the writer in her autobiographical writings as Ugo Tarchetti and Verga's *Storia di una capinera*. Neera's literary style evolves from the romanticism of her early novels and the *verismo* of her production in the 1880s to the idealism of her later production. In novels such as *Nel sogno* (In the dream, 1893), *Anima sola* (One soul, 1895), *L'amuleto* (1897) and *La vecchia casa* (1900), Neera represents an internal female reality, such as the yearning for the ideals of platonic love, maternity and spiritual elevation. In the above-mentioned novels, she abandons the *verist* narrative techniques that characterized novels such as *Teresa* in favor of a literary style aimed at capturing the profoundly intimate essence of her characters' existences. Neera's production evolves throughout her career, undergoing the influence of changing literary trends and revealing an understanding of art as necessarily innovative.

Arslan suggests that Neera's changing literary style damaged her reputation in later years and constitutes the reason for her absence from the Italian literary canon as a quality writer:

> Questo fatto le nocque moltissimo dopo la sua morte, tanto che, sulla base di alcuni romanzi di grande successo popolare ma di scarsa tenuta nel tempo, come *Addio!, La Regaldina, Duello d'anime, Rogo d'amore,* fu possibile farla passare per decenni per una scrittrice "rosa," sentimentale e generica, e assimilarla in tutto a quelle operose artigiane della penna dal lieto fine assicurato che facevano la fortuna delle varie "Biblioteche delle Signorine," travolgendola poi come loro in un'impietosa e ingiusta oscurità. (*Dame, galline e regine* 125–126)[26]

Another factor in my opinion that contributed to overlooking the quality of Neera's *verist* works can be found in Benedetto Croce's appraisal of her later production. Although the esteemed critic demonstrates, in his reviews dedicated to *veristi* Verga and Capuana, a certain appreciation of *verismo*'s faithful representation of reality, he ultimately denies the aesthetic qualities of the movement: "Certamente questo loro programma era sbagliato: la scienza e l'arte sono inconciliabili, non perché avverse ma perché diverse. [Certainly this program of theirs was wrong: science and art are irreconcilable, not because they are adverse but because they are different] (*La Letteratura della nuova Italia* 4: 190). Croce develops a fundamental notion of his aesthetics in the understanding of art's lyrical and individualistic nature, which leads him to reject the impersonal aspect of *verist* art. In his 1903 *La Critica* article dedicated to Verga, for example, Croce observes that "l'impersonale Verga rivela anche qui la sua personalità, fatta di bontà e di malinconia" [the impersonal Verga reveals also here his personality, made of goodness and melancholy] (*La Letteratura della nuova Italia* 3: 29), negating a fundamental aspect of *verismo* in its principal artistic representative. I argue that Croce's lack of appreciation for *verist* aesthetics led him to overlook the quality of Neera's *verist* production in favor of her later literary production because it followed more closely the critic's poetic ideals.

In the 1905 *La Critica* article dedicated exclusively to Neera, Croce proposes a decisive contrast between her production and that of Capuana:

> Se si volesse trovare al Capuana un contrasto quasi perfetto, si dovrebbe pensare, io credo, ai romanzi e agli altri libri della scrittrice lombarda Neera. … Il Capuana non ha idee, non ha sentimenti dominanti e trascinanti, offre spesso i fatti bruti per quella sola importanza che un fatto ha come fatto: Neera è passionale, sentimentale, moralista, meditativa, e non vede il fatto se non attraverso l'ideale. Il Capuana fa desiderare la lirica: Neera vibra tutta di lirica. (*La Letteratura della nuova Italia* 3: 121)[27]

Croce clarifies that it is not his intention to express a judgment of merit by opposing Capuana to Neera but rather to better differentiate between the literary styles of the two writers. Capuana's production, exemplary of *verist* poetics, represents the antithesis not only of Neera's work, according to Croce, but also that of the critic's idea of *poesia pura* [pure poetry]. In presenting Neera and Capuana as opposites, Croce's article puts into motion for critics a process of identification that juxtaposes Capuana, and by extension the literary movement of *verismo*, with Neera.

Throughout his *La Critica* article on Neera, Croce is concerned with identifying the nature of her concept of ideal and demonstrating its coherency throughout her theoretical and narrative production. Croce emphasizes Neera's objective to view reality through the lens of an ideal, praising above all Neera's morality, which he views as the driving force behind her notion of ideal. Croce examines almost exclusively Neera's fervid activity as a theoretical writer, collected in the volumes *Il libro di mio figlio* (1891), *L'amor platonico* (Platonic love, 1897), *Battaglie per un'idea* (1898) and *Le idee di una donna* (1904), as well as the novels which demonstrate the successful interweaving of her theoretical and narrative production: "i suoi libri teorici sono pieni di aneddoti e schizzi artistici; i suoi lavori d'arte tutti compenetrati di idee" [her theoretical books are full of anecdotes and artistic sketches; her works of art are all permeated with ideas] (*La Letteratura della nuova Italia* 3: 128). The overlapping of ideas between different genres reveals, in Croce's view, "la costanza degl'ideali e delle fonti d'ispirazione" [the constancy of ideals and sources of inspiration] (*La Letteratura della nuova Italia* 3: 135) that characterize Neera's production. Affirming that Neera's observation of reality is never separated from her objective to pursue an ideal, Croce proposes a reading of Neera's novels based on an understanding of the ideal as expressed in her theoretical writings. If we recall that Neera's theoretical production dates from 1891 to 1904, it is evident that Croce's evaluation of her literary production focuses primarily on novels written after 1891, following, therefore, her *verist* period.

Writing in the 1919 preface to Neera's autobiography *Una giovinezza del secolo XIX*, Croce reveals his disappointment at the limited critical attention to her work during her lifetime: "Il pregio, in cui ho sempre tenuto gli scritti di Neera, non ha trovato a dir vero, generale consenso nel nostro mondo letterario, dove a questa scrittrice gentile, austera e nobilissima si assegna di solito un posto assai inferiore al merito" [The esteem, in which I have always held Neera's writings, has not found to say the truth, general consensus in our literary world, where this kind, austere and very noble writer is usually assigned a place much inferior to her merit] (*Neera* 945). With the exception of Luigi Russo's inclusion of Neera in his volume *I narratori* (The narrators, 1919), Croce's call for a reevaluation of her work met with little success among contemporary critics. Croce proposes Neera to the public again in 1942, editing a collection of her novels, short stories and essays for publication by Garzanti as part of a series dedicated to nineteenth-century writers. Once again, Croce's proposal of Neera stimulates little interest in a rediscovery, aside from Guido Piovene's 1943 article "Idee e personaggi di Neera" (Ideas and characters in Neera), in which he essentially confirms Croce's esteem of Neera as "uno dei più completi ed equilibrati ingegni della seconda metà del nostro ottocento" [one of the most complete and balanced minds of the second half of our 19th century] (Piovene 3) and the esteemed critic's appreciation of Neera as a moralistic writer: "Neera ebbe un pregio che si associa alla sua indole di moralista e che la rende moderna e vicina a noi" [Neera had a value associated with her moralistic nature and that makes her modern and close to us](Piovene 3).

In later years, while brief references to Neera appeared in volumes of literary history,[28] it is important to note that critical attention to this woman writer, at least until her "rediscovery" in the 1970s, continued to propose a Crocean interpretation of her work, which positioned her as essentially a moralistic writer to the exclusion not only of the feminist aspect of her narrative but also of the quality of her *verist* production.[29] The brief reference to Neera in Francesco Flora's 1956 *Storia della letteratura italiana* (History of

Italian literature) confirms as much: "Il ritratto letterario di Neera, in una maniera che non mi pare possa subire mutamenti, fu disegnato dal Croce" [The literary portrait of Neera, in a way that I don't think can be changed, was drawn by Croce] (V: 448).

This chapter proposes the reconsideration of the literary portrait of Neera, repositioning her within the literary canon as a *verista* for her significant participation in and contribution to the movement's development. Taking her rightful place alongside fellow male *veristi* as well as fellow *verist* woman writer Serao, Neera should be recognized for offering an additional female perspective within the *verist* context, one focused on examining contemporary women's oppression and marginalization in society.

Notes

1 A shorter and slightly different version of this chapter previously appeared in "Neera the *verist* writer." *Italica,* vol. 81, no. 3, Autumn 2004, pp. 351–366.

2 Capuana's critical volumes *Studi sulla letteratura contemporanea* (1880 and 1882), *Per l'arte* (1885) and *Gli "ismi" contemporanei* (1898) represent essential contributions to the theoretical elaboration of the naturalist movement in Italy. Lauri-Lucente refers to *Giacinta* (1879) as "*verismo*'s first novel" (1973).

3 The mysterious process by which passions knot, intertwine, mature, develop in their underground journey, in their comings and goings that often seem contradictory, will for a long time to come still be the powerful attraction of that psychological phenomenon that forms the subject of a story, and that modern analysis aims to follow with scientific scruple.

4 To the so-called verismo belongs, in a broader sense, that narrative which has focused on the "human document" developing the romantic revolution with scientific intentions. The "human document" could be extracted from any context (aristocratic, bourgeois, populous) as demonstrated by the project of the cycle of "Vinti" conceived by Verga, by the works of Capuana and De Roberto, by Serao's *Paese di Cuccagna* where characters of all social classes have been equally reviewed.

5 Federigo Verdinois, "Un nido" *Corriere del Mattino*, 2 March 1880, p. 4.

6 Did I do right by choosing you as my confessor? Are you so free from all earthly ties that you can act as an impartial judge according to the purest doctrines of the literary church? Alas, you have sinned artistically and you continue, alas, to sin too, as far as your happy condition as a woman allows! Alas, you too have, little by little, let yourself be lured by heresy, I hope unconsciously: and it will be your defense before God!

7 See Verga, *Le novelle* 213.

8 See Arslan 1983, Arslan and Verdirame, "Giovanni Verga e Neera: un carteggio" and Arslan and Verdirame "Neera a De Roberto."

9 The tone of the exchange becomes personal as the correspondents switch from the formal *Lei* to the more intimate *Voi.*

10 This reference is from a letter dated August 12, 1911. See Arslan and Verdirame, "Giovanni Verga e Neera: un carteggio" 42.

11 In the years 1880–90, De Roberto is active as a journalist for newspapers such as *Giornale di Sicilia* and *Fanfulla della domenica*. His activity as journalist brings him into contact with Verga and Capuana, with whom he establishes lasting relationships. His literary debut dates to 1887 with the volume of short stories *La Sorte,* and in 1890, he published his first novel *Ermanno Raeli*. His literary success is tied to the novel *I Viceré*, published in 1894.

12 See Federico De Roberto, "Neera" *Giornale di Sicilia*. April 21, 1888.

13 Gerolamo Rovetta (1851–910) is listed by Giulio Ferroni as one of the fin-de-siècle narrators within "un medio orizzonte 'naturalistico.'" See Ferroni 457. Neera's letter to De Roberto refers to the publication in 1892 of his novel *I Barbarò.*

14 Did you hear about Rovetta's triumph with Barbarò? It is a triumph in the family, of which we must all be happy for the love that binds us in the great name of art.

15 See Zambon, "La narrativa realista nei romanzi d'autore di fine Ottocento" 175 for an overview of the critical attention to *Teresa* in late nineteenth-century Italy.

16 The theme of the *zitella* appears in the same years in novels such as Marchesa Colombi's *Un matrimonio in provincia* and Matilde Serao's *Il romanzo della fanciulla.*

17 It was enough for me to see Teresa just once. Pale and sad, sitting apart from her sisters, who joked among themselves, young and cheerful, she sewed a shirt for her distant boyfriend, to whom she had been engaged for ten years, who never came, and whom she always thought about. These two antitheses, his indifference, her constancy: the novel arose whole and vital in a moment.

18 The confusion that must have been produced in your mind with all those characters in the first pages, set out without any presentation as if you had always known them and had been born and lived among them, had to disappear as the reading progressed, to the extent that they returned to you, and affirmed themselves with new actions but without staging, simply, naturally, it was an attempted and sought artifice to avoid, forgive me the pun, any literary artifice, to give you the complete illusion of reality.

19 Aunt Rosa, in the serene placidity of a plant's life, retained some of the statuesque beauty that had thrown her into a man's arms at eighteen years of age - without either of them loving each other, because he needed to find a wife to look after the shop; and she was a girl of marrying age.

20 How white her arms were! She had never had time to look at them, and they appeared to her now as the arms of another person, so thin, round and white. She just couldn't understand how white they were, while the complexion of her face tended to brown, and her neck was brown too; it was only below the collarbone, where her chest began, that white reappeared. This inequality of her skin surprised her; it certainly should

not have been normal. Then, suddenly, she was assailed by a strange thought. Was it good or bad?

21 And Teresina, meanwhile, thought that since they had sent Carlino to Parma, because of high school, and every month it was necessary to pay the pension, there was a lot of talk about economics in her house - and they no longer had a maid - and she had been waiting three months for a new pair of boots.

22 In the Introduction to *I Malavoglia,* Verga uses the term "vinti" to refer to the protagonists of his planned series of five novels. See Verga, *I Malavoglia* 3–7.

23 The woman, for the analytic and sentimental writer, is the subject of predilection, the inexhaustible source of sympathy and art. To mention only the Goncourt brothers, they have seven novels that bear the title of a woman's name, which focus on women and branch out through all the more subtle and more complicated meanders of feminine sensations. Neera refers to the novels *Germinie Lacerteux, Madame Gervasais, Renée Mauperin, Manette Salomon, Soeur Philomène, Chérie* and *La fille Élise.*

24 We bring to the light of day those who have been abandoned and unfortunate and present them to your mercy. ...the cause that most needs this patient work is the cause of the woman. ... I was called unjust, pessimistic, partisan of my sex, when in works written with the most ardent love of my neighbour I dared to defend the woman, the pure woman, the fallen woman, the one who loves and the one who does not love, the woman who is always, for what is woman, oppressed. The article "Le donne che piangono" was originally published in *Fanfulla della domenica* on 15 April, 1888. Excerpts from the article have been published in Arslan, *Dame, galline e regine* 59.

25 To speak only of my literary personality, I observe with wonder that almost all my contemporaries have stalled or fallen asleep and many have fossilized on the first form of their ideal. I have already made two evolutions a while ago, and I have begun the third one in which I am moving forward with an ardor and a freshness that form, for the moment, my greatest happiness.

26 This fact was very much to her detriment after her death, so much so that, on the basis of a number of novels of great popular success, but of little resistance over time, such as *Addio!, La Regaldina, Duello d'anime, Rogo d'amore*, it was possible to make her pass for decades as a "pink," sentimental and generic writer, and to assimilate her in everything to those industrious craftswomen of the pen with an assured happy ending who made the fortune of the various "Libraries of the Ladies," then overwhelming her like them in a pitiless and unjust darkness.

27 If one wanted to find for Capuana an almost perfect contrast, one would have to think, I believe, of the novels and other books by the Lombard writer Neera. Capuana has no ideas, he has no dominant and compelling feelings, he often offers brute facts for the only importance that a fact has as a fact: Neera is passionate, sentimental, moralistic, meditative, and does not see the fact except through the ideal. Capuana makes one long for lyricism: Neera vibrates with lyricism.

28 See Cattaneo 269–488. Cattaneo refers to Neera as a "scrittirce moralista" who privileges in her literary production "i sacrifici anonimi, le rinunce senza strepito, gli slanci non gridati" (400).
29 See Russo 138, Piovene 3, Cattaneo 400, Borlenghi 329 and Flora 448.

References

Arslan, Antonia. *Dame, galline e regine. La scrittura femminile italiana fra '800 e '900*, edited by Marina Pasqui, Milan, Guerini, 1998.

———. "Luigi Capuana e Neera: Corrispondenza inedita 1881–1885." *Miscellanea di studi in onore di Vittore Branca*. Florence, Olschki, 1983, pp. 161–185.

——— and Patrizia Zambon, editors. *Il sogno aristocratico. Angiolo Orvieto e Neera. Corrispondenza 1889–1917.* Milan, Guerini, 1990.

——— and Rita Verdirame. "Giovanni Verga e Neera: un carteggio." *Quaderni di filologia e letteratura siciliana*, vol. 5, 1978, pp. 27–42.

——— and Rita Verdirame. "Neera a De Roberto." *Archivio storico per la Sicilia Orientale*, vol. LXVIII, 1982, pp. 249–270.

Baldacci, Luigi. Introduction. *Teresa*, by Neera. Turin, Einaudi, 1976, pp. v–xii.

Baldi, Guido. *L'artificio della regressione. Tecnica narrativa e ideologia nel Verga verista*. Naples, Liguori, 1980.

Borlenghi, Aldo. *Narratori dell'Ottocento e del primo Novecento*. Milan, Ricciardi, 1966.

Capuana, Luigi. "A Neera." Preface. *Giacinta*. 3rd ed., Catania 1889, Florence, Valecchi, 1972, pp. 29–38.

———."Come io divenni novelliere. Confessione a Neera." Preface. *Homo*. 2nd ed., Milano, Treves, 1888, pp. v–xxxv.

———.*Giacinta*. Milan, Mondadori, 1980.

———. *Per l'arte*. 1885. Naples, Edizioni scientifiche italiane, 1994.

———. *Studii sulla letteratura contemporanea*, edited by Paola Azzolini, Naples, Liguori, 1988.

Cattaneo, Giulio. "Prosatori e critici della Scapigliatura al Verismo." *Storia della letteratura italiana*, edited by Emilio Cecchi and Natalio Sapegno, vol. 8, Milan, Garzanti, 1968, pp. 269–488.

Cecchetti, Giovanni. "La 'Nedda' del Verga." *Belfagor*, vol. 15, no. 3, 31 May 1960, pp. 270–283.

Croce, Benedetto. *La letteratura della nuova Italia*. Bari, Laterza, 1948.

———, editor. *Neera*. Milan, Garzanti, 1942.

De Benedetti, Giacomo. *Verga e il naturalismo*. Milan, Garzanti, 1976.

De Roberto, Federico. "Neera." *Giornale di Sicilia*, 21 April, 1888.

Ferroni, Giulio. *Storia della letteratura italiana. Dall'Ottocento al Novecento*. Turin, Einaudi, 1991.

Flora, Francesco. *Storia della letteratura italiana*. Milan, Mondadori, 1962.

Lauri-Lucente, Gloria. "Verismo." Encyclopedia of Italian Literary Studies, edited by Gaetana Marrone. New York, Routledge, 2007, pp. 172–75.
Madrignani, Carlo A. *Capuana e il naturalismo.* Bari, Laterza, 1970.
Mitchell, Katharine. *Italian Women Writers: Gender and Everyday Life in Fiction and Journalism, 1870–1910.* Toronto, U of Toronto P, 2014.
Neera. *Confessioni letterarie. Neera*, edited by Benedetto Croce, Milan, Garzanti, 1942, pp. 871–809.
———. *Teresa*, edited by Luigi Badacci, Turin, Einaudi, 1976.
———. *Una giovinezza del secolo XIX.* Milan, Cogliati, 1919.
Nicolosi, Francesco. *Questioni verghiane.* Rome, Ateneo, 1969.
Pellini, Pierluigi. *Naturalismo e verismo.* Florence, La Nuova Italia, 1998.
Piovene, Guido. "Idee e personaggi di Neera." *Corriere della sera*, 20 May, 1943, p. 3.
Russo, Luigi. *I Narratori.* Milan, Giuseppe Principato, 1951.
Valisa, Silvia. "Cosa scrivevano le donne di fine Ottocento? Il contributo italiano alla Woman's Building Library della World Fair di Chicago (1893)." *Gender/Sexuality/Italy*, vol. 5, August 2018, pp. 236–256.
Verga, Giovanni. *I grandi romanzi*, edited by Ferrucco Cecco and Carlo Riccardi. Milan, Mondadori, 1972.
———. *I Malavoglia.* Turin, Einaudi, 1997.
———. *Le novelle*, vol. 1, Milan, Garzanti, 1983.
———. *Lettere a Luigi Capuana*, edited by Gino Raya, Florence, Le Monnier, 1975.
Zola, Émile. *Le Roman Expérimental.* Paris, Charpentier, 1881.
———. *Thérèse Raquin.* Paris, Charpentier, 1922.

4 Letter Writing

A Tool of the Trade for Italian Women Writers

Neera's archive, defined by Antonia Arslan as "uno degli archivi più ricchi e completi del nostro tardo Ottocento e del primo Novecento" [one of the richest and most complete archives of the late 19th - early 20th century period] (Arslan and Pasqui 31), and the publication of many of her *epistolari* [epistolary correspondences] have shed further light on the development of this writer's literary style as well as on her prominent role in literary, journalistic and cultural circles of the time.[1] In this chapter, I will examine how Neera's numerous letter exchanges with leading figures from fin-de-siècle Italian literary, artistic and editorial circles provide a better understanding of this complex figure and her literary production. The following figure among the novelists with whom Neera corresponded: Luigi Capuana, Giovanni Verga, Matilde Serao, Federico De Roberto, Roberto Bracco, Luigi Pirandello, Antonio Fogazzaro, Paolo Mantegazza, Emanuele Navarro della Miraglia and Tommaso Cannizarro.[2] She corresponded with literary critics and representatives from editorial and journalistic spheres, such as Benedetto Croce, Vittorio Pica, Federigo Verdinois, George Hérelle, Ferdinand Brunetière, Edouard Rod, Gustavo Botta, Giuseppe Saverio Gargàno, Jakša Čedomil and Leone Fortis. Letter exchanges with young, emerging writers such as Angiolo Orvieto, Filippo Tommaso Marinetti, Marino Moretti, Ada Negri and Vittoria Aganoor testify to Neera's interest in *letterati nuovi* [new writers]. Her epistolary exchanges extended also outside literary circles to include figurative artists such as Giovanni Segantini, Giuseppe Pellizza da Volpedo and Vittore Grubicy de Dragon. Neera's varied and extensive epistolary exchanges complete an understanding of this fin-de-siècle woman writer's multi-faceted personality and diverse literary production, as Arslan suggests:

> Emerge da queste corrispondenze una Neera segreta che integra e completa l'immagine un po' reticente e contradditoria

> che si ricava dalle sue opere pubblicate, dove si alternano, in anni a volte molto vicini fra loro, prese di posizione e affermazioni di carattere che oggi si direbbe decisamente "reazionario" e altre sottilmente coraggiose e – per quell'epoca – anche audaci, o romanzi schiettamente naturalistici, come *Teresa*, e altri di impronta esasperatamente idealistica, come *Nel sogno*. (Dame, galline e regine 88)[3]

The diversified and at times contrasting positions adopted by Neera in her epistolary exchanges offer a more complete picture of the variegated contexts in which fin-de-siècle women writers lived and worked.

Letter Writing: A Communicative Tool in Fin-de-Siècle Italy

Letter writing as an everyday communicative tool became a characteristic, even a social necessity, of middle-class, late nineteenth-century Italian society, as Gabriella Romani discusses in *Postal Culture: Writing and Reading Letters in Post-Unification Italy* (2013):

> Obviously, people did not begin writing letters in the nineteenth century, but it is only at this moment of the convergence of different economic, social, and cultural phenomena – with growing literacy rates, a wider newspaper circulation, and a more reliable postal service – that letter writing became an everyday practice. (24)

Technological advancements within post-Unification Italy, such as improved railway systems; the electric telegraph; and, for the first time, a nationalized postal service, allowed for a substantial increase in the use of letter writing as a form of communication in everyday life, for personal as well as business affairs. In "Riviste Fiorentine e Milanesi dell'ultimo Ottocento nel carteggio Angiolo Orvieto-Neera" (Late 19th- century Florentine and Milanese journals in the Angiolo Orvieto-Neera correspondence, 1990) Patrizia Zambon refers to Neera's epistolary exchanges as a "strumento di lavoro" [working tool], noting the communicative function she reserved for each one, regardless of the nature of her relationship with the correspondent (33–35). The work element is almost always present in Neera's letter exchanges, such as requesting or offering literary reviews and advice or help with a publication. In the article

"Lettere" (Letters), published in 1911 in *Il Marzocco*, Neera reveals her appreciation of the purely functional nature of the epistolary genre:

> Un ramo letterario dei più interessanti è quello che raccoglie gli Epistolari, quantunque le lettere private non entrino che di straforo a far parte della letteratura propriamente detta essendo la lettera in genere non una manifestazione di studio e di dottrina ma il semplice adempimento di una funzione sociale.[4]

Neera recognizes the intimacy of the epistolary exchange as a literary form constructed by two voices, where each letter exists in relation to a response in a private exchange. The letter offers her a space in which she can express herself free from stylistic constraints and concerns. In a 1911 letter to poet Marino Moretti, Neera acknowledges the difficulty she experiences as a self-educated writer in expressing herself in a language that often required study and concentration: "I critici fecero sempre a me tanti appunti sulla forma che ho dovuto riconoscerne l'importanza ed è per questo che mi permetto di metterla in guardia" [The critics always made so many notes on my form that I had to recognize its importance and that's why I warn you] (Zambon and Pegoraro 63). While Neera expresses concern about the language and style of her literary works, she reserves an intimate and personal function for her epistolary writing, as she reveals in another letter to Moretti: "È questa l'ora dei miei ricevimenti intimi; l'ora cioè in cui perfettamente libera e sola, nel silenzio del mio salottino, apro il cuore a chi voglio"[5] [This is the hour of my intimate receptions; that is, the hour when perfectly free and alone, in the silence of my sitting room, I open my heart to whomever I want]. Arslan notes that it is "proprio nella scrittura epistolare che le nostre scrittrici fra Otto e Novecento si liberano dunque meglio e meglio seguono, con felice aderenza dello stile al pensiero, il loro io profondo e le ragioni peculiari delle loro scelte" [precisely in epistolary writing that our turn-of-the-century women writers liberate themselves better and therefore follow better, with a happy adherence of style to thought, their deep self and the peculiar reasons for their choices] (Arslan and Zambon 15).

While Neera privileges the privacy of the epistolary genre for its functionality, informality and intimacy, Diane Cousineau argues in *Letters and Labyrinths: Women Writing/Cultural Codes* (1997) that the letter is an emblem of the tension between private and public spheres, suggesting that "at once a vehicle of the most personal and private reflections, it is also a reminder that all human discourse is regulated by public codes and channels and thus subject to institutional control" (16). Even within the setting of Neera's private letters, it is possible to find instances which display her awareness of her own public persona as well as that of her addressee. The use of her pseudonym in her epistolary exchanges, private exchanges not meant for publication, and the almost complete elimination of any mention of personal or family affairs point to Neera's awareness of the letter as more than just a moment for opening her heart. Cousineau notes that

> [p]erhaps more than any other genre, the letter blatantly speaks of the irremediable division of the self, on the level of both the Imaginary and the Symbolic; its incapacity to be true to, or consistent with, itself. … The addressee is no less an invention and projection of the writer than is the addresser, and so phantom speaks to phantom. (30–31)

Through my analysis of Neera's numerous epistolary correspondences, I will examine the writer's multi-faceted personality that emerges and the wide range of positions she adopts, from declarations of solidarity or displays of acquiescence to authority to the authoritative defense of her views. In her epistolary exchanges with the established and esteemed literary critics and writers Croce, Botta and Capuana, Neera plays the role of the uncertain woman writer seeking guidance and assurance from a fatherly figure. However, in epistolary exchanges with the directors of the journals *Pungolo* and *Revue des Deux Mondes*, Neera is not afraid to stand up for her rights and defend her views on the quality of her production. At other times, Neera takes on the role of guide, providing maternal instruction and encouragement for budding young writers and critics, as in her epistolary exchanges with Moretti, Angiolo Orvieto and Jakša Čedomil. The letters to Neera from women writers Matilde Serao, Ada Negri and Vittoria Aganoor reveal a shared solidarity based on their shared role as woman writers, alluding to the desire in those years for a female network of collaboration. Alberto Vecchi notes that letters represent the "documenti del tessuto culturale o morale che retrostà alle persone e che sembra utile rilevare, per far meglio conoscere il valore storico delle persone stesse" [documents of the cultural or moral fabric behind people and that it seems useful to highlight, to make better known the historical value of the people themselves] (56). The various attitudes and roles adopted by Neera in her epistolary exchanges reveal the inaccuracy of blindly categorizing women writers as emarginated, oppressed or obsequious in their relations and interactions with figures of the literary world. Like any writer seeking to protect her interests and aware of what she stands to lose or gain, Neera conducts her letter exchanges accordingly. Romani argues that

> [a]s a means of connection in a complex of cultural and social intersections, the letter reveals the hidden dynamics and intricate interplay existing among the different interlocutors or cultural subjects (authors, critics, publishers, and readers) who inhabited and influenced a literary period still too often critically assessed through the exclusive study of single figures or ideas. (11)

Through the reconstruction of the faceted aspects of Neera's personality as they emerge from her epistolary exchanges, it is possible to reconstruct a complete picture, not only of her personality and experiences as woman and writer, but also of the period in which she was active.

Exchanges with Literary Father Figures

Neera adopts a "daughterly" role in her epistolary exchanges with esteemed male writers and literary critics Capuana, Verga, Croce, Botta[6] and Gargàno.[7] In the context of these letter exchanges, Neera plays the part of the unassured woman writer seeking evaluation, approval and confirmation of her work from writers and critics whom she regards as authoritative. Neera's reverent and submissive attitude cannot be attributed to merely a question of age, for she was older than Croce, Botta and Gargàno. Nor is Neera's attitude merely linked to the uncertainties of a writer in the early phase of their literary career. Although Neera's exchanges with Capuana and Verga take place in the early years of her career, 1881–85, those with Croce, Botta and Gargàno occur in its final phase, from 1898 onward. Regardless of her age, experience and literary success, Neera's letter exchanges with Capuana, Verga, Croce, Botta and Gargàno reveal her lack of faith in the stylistic quality of her production and lack of confidence in her critical ability to evaluate her own production. Arslan notes Neera's "estenuante ricerca – durata tutta la vita – di un 'padre intellettuale' a cui appoggiarsi, che … si dimostrasse disposto a fornirle una 'filosofia' di base, un sostegno strutturato di idee, capace di dare giustificazione teorica allo spontaneo organizzarsi del suo talento narrativo" [a tireless life-long search for an "intellectual father" to lean on, who ... would be willing to provide her with a basic "philosophy," a structured system of ideas, capable of giving theoretical justification to the spontaneous organization of her narrative talent] (*Dame, galline e regine* 126). Given her declared devotion toward her own father, upon whom she modeled several of the father figures in her novels, as discussed previously in this study, it is not surprising to find the projection of a similar father-daughter dynamic in her epistolary writing. Neera's exchanges with esteemed male writers reveal how women writers were at times dependent upon their male counterparts for guidance regarding their literary style and for help in publishing and ensuring the public's approval of their works.

In her exchanges with the "father" figures examined, Neera emphasizes her desire for a sincere and honest evaluation of her work, rather than merely superficial approval, as the following excerpt from a letter to Capuana dated March 30, 1884 reveals: "l'avrei in mala parte l'applauso cieco dell'affetto e della simpatia – offa che molti palati ingoiano con delizia, ma io no. Verità vo cercando che è sì cara – null'altro" [I look down on the blind applause of affection and sympathy – a reward that many palates swallow with delight, but I don't. I seek truth, it is so precious - nothing else] (Arslan, "Luigi Capuana e Neera" 173). Other examples include, roughly 20 years later, a letter to Gargàno in 1903, in which Neera writes, "Non chiedo lode, chiedo attenzione" [I don't ask for praise, but rather attention] (Brotto 179), and a letter to Botta in 1906, in which she requests that he give her "francamente la sua opinione" [your frank opinion] (Martini 199), revealing her ongoing search for guidance during her long literary career. On several occasions in her correspondences with these writers, Neera willingly adopts the role of a student who has much to learn and who seeks the instruction of a teacher. She clarifies her role in her relationship with Capuana in a letter dated December 12, 1882, when she states regarding his fable "La Reginotta": "Lei capirà che la scolara non può criticare il maestro" [You will understand that the schoolgirl cannot criticize the teacher] (Arslan, "Luigi Capuana e Neera" 170). More than 20 years later, in her correspondence with Botta, Neera again takes on the role of student, anxious to learn from his advice: "Vuol leggere il pezzettino di prosa che le accludo? La prima volta che ci vedremo mi saprà poi dire se è stile. Faccio il possibile, come vede, per approfittare delle sue lezioni!" [Would you like to read the little piece of prose I'm enclosing? The first time we meet, you'll be able to tell me if it's style. I do everything I can, as you see, to take advantage of your lessons!] (Martini 197). Other examples can be found in her correspondence with Croce, which dates principally from the years surrounding the writing and publication of his 1905 *La Critica* article on Neera. Her letters reveal complete acceptance of and submission to the critic's evaluation of her production. On more than one occasion, Neera acknowledges Croce's approval of her work as that which represents her maximum goal as writer, as in the following letter dated March 31, 1904: "L'approvazione di una persona come Lei sarebbe per me il più ambito usbergo ai colpi che non mancheranno di scoccarmi i miei avversari" [The approval of a person like you would be for me the most sought-after armor against the blows that my opponents will not fail to strike me] (Arslan and Folli 53). The above examples reveal not only Neera's uncertainty regarding her literary style but also her desire to adhere to determined stylistic standards.

In several cases, Neera seeks advice from the above-mentioned father figures on how to improve her literary style. Throughout her career, Neera faced accusations of poor literary style, initially defending herself from such criticisms by proclaiming her belief in the supremacy of content over form. After the publication of Croce's *La Critica* article, which pointed out stylistic weaknesses in her work, Neera began to dedicate more attention to her literary style, as evidenced in her letter exchanges with Croce, Botta and Gargàno, all of which date from the final phase of her career. Neera "confesses" her faults and weaknesses to Croce, acknowledging the defects of her literary form: "ma che cosa sperare se mi manca addirittura il mezzo primo per scrivere?" [but what can I hope for if I do not even have the first tool to write?] (Arslan and Folli 67). She turns to Botta as a guide in her search to develop a more sophisticated style of writing in a letter dated May 4, 1908:

> Le voglio anche dire che in tutto questo tempo che non ci vediamo ho pensato a lei e precisamente tutte le volte che mi trovavo alle prese col nuovo romanzo che langue da parecchi mesi sul mio scrittoio, paralizzato da una singolare lentezza di esecuzione. Sono diventata difficile e combatto anch'io strenuamente, nel mio piccolo, per la ricerca del vocabolo – non prezioso ma esatto. (Martini 202)[8]

Botta's work represented for Neera a stylistic model that she struggled to achieve, as numerous references in her letters to her continued attempts at stylistic improvement reveal.

Neera's exchange with Gargàno provides further examples of her search for improvement in her literary style, in particular her poetic production, which was decidedly minor compared to her narrative and journalistic production. During her literary career, Neera published only one volume of poetry, *Il canzioniere della nonna* (The grandmother's verses, 1908), a collection of 21 poems dedicated to her grandson Corradino Martinelli. In the preface, Neera reveals an understanding of poetry as a genre suitable for the immediate expression of her spirit, defending her view of poetry "nel suo significato primitivo di slancio e di prorompimento dell'animo fuori dalle dighe comuni" [in its primitive meaning of momentum and soul-bursting from the common dams] (*Il canzoniere della nonna* 8). In another passage from the preface to *Il canzoniere della nonna,* she acknowledges her search for a poetic language different from that of her narrative production:

> Sento questo bisogno di parlare in certi momenti una lingua diversa, più ampia, più armoniosa, che abbia la leggerezza del volo e la sonorità dell'eco, che palpiti come un'ala e gema come una fonte e si corruschi di mille iridescenze come un raggio di sole attraverso una goccia di rugiada... (Il canzoniere della nonna 8)[9]

Denying any poetic pretensions for the poems, Neera describes them rather as a "miracolo d'amore" [a miracle of love] (Neera, *Il canzoniere della nonna* 10). However, it is precisely her search for a more sophisticated poetic mode of expression that leads Neera to turn to Gargàno for advice and approval. In a letter dated July 15, 1898, she asks the critic for his evaluation of a group of poems she sent him, revealing her need for reassurance regarding her poetry:

> Non [intendo] nulla della poesia, non conosco la metrica, sono una perfetta ignorante; pure non so perché in certi rari istanti della vita mi sgorgano dal cuore quelle righe corte tutte piene delle mie lacrime e dei miei sogni. Vorrei sapere se in esse c'è qualche cosa che valga la pena di rimanere. Io sono, le ripeto, così incompetente in materia che m'è impossibile giudicare da me. (Brotto 170)[10]

Gargàno responds by recognizing and praising Neera's ability to convey emotion in her poetry, correctly identifying a fundamental aspect of Neera's writing, whether it be narrative, poetic or theoretical, in the desire to express love and passion.

Neera's letter exchanges with esteemed literary father figures reveal not only her search for approval and advice but also her attempts to seek help in publishing her works. In a letter to Verga dated November 25, 1884, Neera requests advice in publishing her latest novel, *Il marito dell'amica*, having recently signed a contract with an editor on the verge of bankruptcy:

> Navarro,[11] da Roma, mi ha fatto concludere un contratto col Sommaruga per la pubblicazione di un mio romanzo nel prossimo futuro Natale. Questo, quattro giorni fa. In questi quattro giorni, a farlo apposta, mi piovono da ogni parte notizie allarmanti e disonorevoli per il Sommaruga e per chi scrive con lui. Io vivo così fuori del mondo, e sono poco, così poco pratica delle sue cabale, che mi trovo imbarazzatissima. ... Lei deve conoscere la cosa. Mi dice una sola parola – rompo o no?[12] (Arslan and Verdirame, "Giovanni Verga e Neera" 37)

Neera reveals her reliance on the advice of esteemed male colleagues for help in navigating the complex world of publishing. In a letter to Capuana dated July 20, 1882, she grants the critic the right to decide the conclusion of the short story *Angelica* she sent him for publication in *Fanfulla della domenica*: "Osservi il segno che ho fatto all'ultimo periodo perché sono incerta se lasciarlo oppure terminare il bozzetto alla parola forestiero. E di questo la lascio arbitro" [Observe the mark I made at the last period because I am uncertain whether to leave it or finish the draft with the word foreigner. And regarding this I leave the decision up to you] (Arslan, "Luigi Capuana e Neera" 169). The short story was, in fact, published in the July 30, 1882, issue of *Fanfulla della domenica* ending with the word *forestiero*. In another letter to Capuana dated November 25, 1882, Neera acknowledges her sense of uncertainty within journalistic circles, offering further insight into her desire for guidance: "Il Fanfulla della domenica mi ha sempre fatto paura ed anche questo è un motivo che mi paralizza; temo sempre che l'articolo non sia adatto" [Fanfulla della domenica has always scared me and this is also a reason that paralyzes me; I'm always afraid that the article is not suitable] (Arslan, "Luigi

Capuana e Neera" 169). Neera reveals in a very open and candid manner her feelings of insecurity regarding her judgment and the worth of her production. More than 20 years later, in a letter to Croce dated October 31, 1903, she again expresses her willingness to accept the critic's evaluation of her work, blindly acquiescing to his judgment: "Il mio poco criterio critico non mi lascia decidere nella varietà de' miei libri quale prevalga del realismo e dell'idealismo. Basta; lei giudicherà e la parola sua mi servirà di faro" [My limited critical judgment does not allow me to determine in which of my books prevails realism and in which prevails idealism. Enough; you will judge, and your word will serve me as a beacon] (Arslan and Folli 51). Neera looks to Croce as an authority in interpreting the stylistic qualities of her own production, again revealing her lack of self-esteem. In the same year, Neera writes in a letter to Gargàno: "Mi trovo in un momento di sfiducia; ho bisogno che una coscienza intelligente mi dica con tutta franchezza se sono uno scrittore o se sono un'imbecille" [I am in a moment of doubt; I need an intelligent conscience to tell me frankly whether I am a writer or an imbecile] (Brotto 177). The momentary lack of self-confidence referenced in the letter can be linked perhaps to the negative reviews her latest novel *Una passione* had received.[13] The following passage from Neera's article "La donna scrittrice" (The woman writer) reveals her understanding of how a writer's sense of accomplishment was inevitably linked to public recognition and success:

> Vi sentite solo, solo con [il vostro libro], col vostro sogno, colla vostra illusione, colla vostra passione; solo nell'ampio mondo che non vi guarda, che non si interessa affatto a ciò che avete scritto per lui, che non si cura per nulla dei vostri pensieri e delle vostre convinzioni; che lavora, mangia, dorme, va a spasso, si diverte, si annoia, sta bene, sta male, lungi, ben lungi da voi e dalle vostre fantasime. E vi abbattete intontito e grullo sulla vetrina dove il vostro libro giace nella immobilità tragica dei morti. (Le idee di una donna 830)[14]

Neera's correspondences with established and respected male writers and literary critics confirm the difficulties of the literary profession for many women writers, uncertain of their literary worth and how to navigate literary circles, and the benefit and at times necessity of creating an extensive network of relations in order to succeed.

Defending Poetic Ideals

Neera's letter exchanges also offer evidence of occasions in which she does not submissively accept the guidance of male authority figures, as her correspondences with representatives of journalistic and editorial circles reveal. In her letters to *Pungolo* director Leone Fortis, *Corriere del Mattino Letterario* director Federigo Verdinois, *Vita Nuova* director Angiolo Orvieto and French literary journal *Revue des Deux Mondes* translator George Hérelle, Neera aggressively defends her rights as writer and the quality of her production.

Neera's ties to the literary journal *Pungolo* began in 1875 with the publication of her first novel *Un romanzo.* Her epistolary exchange with Leone Fortis dates from February 1883 to June 1884, and although Neera had already published five novels in 1883 and received the critical attention of critics such as Luigi Capuana, she was still relatively at the beginning of her literary career. Fortis's responses to her letters reveal, however, that she was already fully capable of defending her economic interests when necessary. In a letter dated October 31, 1883, Fortis writes:

> Non so spiegarmi il tono che, se non iscrivessi ad una amabile Signora, direi quasi scortese con cui Ella rispose ieri ai miei eccitamenti per proseguire e terminare la serie dei suoi *bozzetti matrimoniali.* Non credo di aver mancato mai verso di Lei, ai riguardi dovuti ad una colta e gentile Signora, né credo vi abbia mai mancato il giornale. Ignoro se l'amministrazione, in questi mesi di assenze frequenti e di occupazioni accresciute, e di asciutte estive, le abbia ritardato qualche pagamento – ma so che il suo conto è completamente saldato – per cui il ritardo non può essere stato che di breve entità. (Collino Pansa, "Piccolo viaggio in un archivio" 256)[15]

Fortis's reference to Neera's impolite tone allows us to understand that she did not hesitate to demand compensation for a previous collaboration before proceeding with new work, revealing a forwardness that must have been unusual for a *signora* of the time. Fortis's answer to Neera's following letter reveals a justification for the impolite tone of her previous letter: "Facciamo la pace – o per meglio dire, la faccia col mio Amministratore, il quale è un buon figliolo a cui non è mai passata per capo la brutta e villana idea di *abusare della sua debolezza di donna e della sua posizione di scrittrice*" [Let's make peace - or rather, make peace with my administrator, who is a good boy who has never had the ugly and vile idea of taking advantage of your weakness as a woman and your position as a woman writer] (Collino Pansa, "Piccolo viaggio in un archivio" 256). Fortis's apparent citation from Neera's previous letter reveals her awareness of how contemporary perceptions of women as inferior, as discussed in the Introduction to this study, created difficulties for women writers within the male-dominated literary and journalistic circles of fin-de-siècle Italy. Neera was careful to protect her interests against those who might try to take advantage of her "condition" as woman and woman writer.

Neera's letter exchange with Federigo Verdinois, director of *Corriere del Mattino*'s Sunday insert *Corriere del Mattino Letterario*, demonstrates that her sensitivity regarding her status as a woman writer was not unfounded. On September 6, 1877, Verdinois responds to a letter from Neera in which presumably she had requested clarification on the direction of the two publications, evidently also complaining about problems she had experienced in having her articles published in *Corriere del Mattino*. After declaring *Corriere del Mattino Letterario* to be independent and separate from *Corriere del Mattino* and in an evident attempt to entice Neera's collaboration, Verdinois reveals a possible reason for her difficulty in publishing with *Corriere del Mattino*:

> Non mi sorprende che non abbiano pubblicato qualche suo scritto; non l'avranno capito; non sanno che valore abbiano gli altri scritti da lei pubblicati. Mancano di rispetto ad una donna e ad un'artista. Queste cose le dico in confidenza, cogliendo questa occasione per esprimerle tutta la mia ammirazione. (Arslan, "Neera e il giornalismo napoletano" 593)[16]

The references to and distinctions between *donna/signora* and *scrittrice/artista*, noted in Verdinois's and Fortis's letters, reveal the pervasiveness of conceptions regarding women writers as divided between home and profession and the expectations for them to behave according to established modes of social conduct for women. Neera reveals a combativeness in her business correspondences that contrasted with such modes of conduct. In another letter, responding frankly to Neera's apparent demand to know the reasons for the delay in publishing her articles, Verdinois writes: "Parlerò anch'io chiaro. Il ritardo frapposto alla pubblicazione dei suoi articoli è tutto colpa mia. Il pagamento degli articoli lo fo *io*, ed è per questo che indugiavo la pubblicazione, temendo non m'avesse ella a richiedere del pronto pagamento" [I'll speak plainly, too. The delay in publishing your articles is all my fault. I paid for the articles, and that's why I was delaying the publication, fearing that you would ask me to pay promptly] (Arslan, "Neera e il giornalismo napoletano" 595). Verdinois's responses to Neera's letters demonstrate that she exhibited the same tenacity to protect her interests as writer as that already noted in her correspondence with Fortis. Neera's correspondences with Fortis and Verdinois reveal that writing was not a mere pastime for her, but rather a source of income on which she depended.

In addition to the combative manner she demonstrates regarding financial concerns, Neera also fiercely defends the quality of her production, rejecting attempts to label her work as *letteratura vendereccia* [easy to sell literature] or *letteratura femminile* [female literature]. In a letter to Neera dated November 5, 1877, Verdinois responds to one such defense by Neera: "Non ho mai lontanamente sospettato di lei, quando mi ha parlato di letteratura vendereccia; anch'io vendo come Lei, epperò non avevo il diritto né di sorprendermi né di prendere in mala parte le sue idee economiche" [I never remotely suspected you, when you spoke to me about easy to sell literature; I, too, sell like you, and I had no right to be surprised or to take your economic ideas in bad faith] (Arslan, "Neera e il giornalismo napoletano" 594). In a letter to Angiolo Orvieto dated February 1, 1890, regarding his review of her novel *L'indomani* for the journal *Vita Nuova*,[17] Neera satirically rejects categorization of her work as *letteratura femminile:* "Legga, se ha voglia e tempo, alcuni versi miei che usciranno l'una o l'altra di queste domeniche sul Fanfulla letterario. Vedrà che ci si trova della psicologia non esclusivamente femminile" [Read, if you have the will and the time, some verses of mine that will come out one or the other of these Sundays on the Fanfulla letterario. You will see that there is some psychology that is not exclusively feminine] (Arslan and Zambon 57). In the same letter, she criticizes not only *Vita Nuova*'s superficial attention to her novel but also the journal's lack of consideration for contemporary Italian literary production in general:

> Quando uscì il suo articolo sulla *Vita Nuova* io ero già ammalata; ma se dispiacere vi fu (non ira né vendetta) si riferì solamente alla trascuranza posta nell'occuparsi del mio libro, mentre la *Vita* che si chiama *Nuova* e che dovrebbe essere *italiana* aveva pur dedicato lunghe colonne ai romanzieri d'oltralpe... Sempre così qui da noi. Ci battono, e noi li lecchiamo! (Arslan and Zambon 57)[18]

Unafraid to present her opinion to the journal's director on its negligence in examining and presenting her work to the public, Neera demands her novel's worth alongside that of European authors.

An unpublished letter from Neapolitan journalist Roberto Bracco to Neera reveals her unwillingness to compromise her artistic ideals and standards for anyone, whether it be for a friend or fellow writer, or for any reason, such as publicity or financial retribution.[19] In a letter dated November 14, 1891, Bracco asks Neera to write the preface for a collection of his short stories. Bracco's letter in response acknowledges his decision not to publish Neera's proposed preface[20]: "Mia buona amica – ho letto e riletto la vostra lettera-prefazione, e, naturalmente, ho deciso di non pubblicarla. Essa avrebbe dovuto decidermi altresì a non pubblicare il libro; … Voi, in essa, dimostrate con troppa efficacia la pochezza delle novelline e la pochezza mia" [My good friend - I have read and reread your letter-preface, and of course I decided not to publish it. It should also have convinced me not to publish the book; ... In it you demonstrate too effectively the smallness of the novels and my smallness] (Saladino 206). Bracco's letter indicates Neera's refusal to compromise her poetic ideals by writing a complimentary preface to a work that she does not truly appreciate, as a later letter by Bracco confirms, when he writes that Neera's artistic ideals prevent her from recognizing that "anche l'essenza umana di molte cose brutte o mediocri o piccini può essere oggetto d'arte" [also the human essence of many ugly or mediocre or small things can be the object of art] (Saladino 210). Neera and Bracco's exchange demonstrates her refusal to accommodate a fellow writer by compromising her literary views, even if it means disappointing a friend and fellow writer and renouncing an opportunity for visibility for herself.

An episode that perhaps best demonstrates Neera's staunch defense of her poetic ideal within the competitive literary profession comes from her epistolary exchange regarding the translation and publication of *L'indomani* in the French literary journal *Revue des Deux Mondes*. In February 1898, George Hérelle, translator for the French journal, offered to translate *L'indomani*, one of a group of novels sent to him by Neera for consideration. Arslan notes the importance of such an opportunity for an Italian writer in that period: "Pubblicare in Francia, essere tradotti a Parigi costituiva in quegli anni la massima aspirazione di un letterato italiano" [To publish in France, to be translated in Paris was in those years the greatest aspiration of an Italian writer] (*Dame, galline e regine* 119). It is important to note that very few Italian writers succeeded in finding success in French literary circles. Gabriele D'Annunzio and Matilde Serao were among a select few whose works were translated in those years by Hérelle for publication in the prestigious *Revue des Deux Mondes*. In her *carteggio* with literary critic Vittorio Pica,[21] Neera discusses her attempts to publish in France in the 1890s. In a letter to Neera on September 24, 1894, Pica responds to her request for help in getting her works translated for publication abroad by revealing the difficulty of the endeavor:

> Per le traduzioni, alla Francia non bisogna pensare: Verga e Fogazzaro non vi hanno ottenuto alcun successo e se D'Annunzio è piaciuto ciò devesi non soltanto al suo eccezionale valore artistico, ma anche e sopra tutto alla sua psicologia sottile, raffinata, ed un po' morboso in accordo con le più recenti squisite tendenze della giovane letteratura d'oltralpe. (Finotti 142)[22]

Pica reveals the challenging task of getting published in France for even two of the most successful writers of the time, Giovanni Verga and Antonio Fogazzaro. For the honor of being published in France's most prestigious journal, or as the journal's translator Hérelle writes to Neera, "la première de France, - et un francais serait tenté de dire: du monde!" [the best in France, - and a Frenchman would be tempted to say: in the world!] (Arslan *Dame, galline e regine* 124), many writers granted the journal full liberty in translating and editing their works. During the preparation of *L'indomani* for publication, Hérelle justifies the necessary adaptations of her novel for publication in *Revue des Deux Mondes* in a letter to Neera on November 14, 1899:

> Songez: 1) que les lecteurs d'une Revue ne sont pas des lecteurs ordinaires … 2) que votre livre, paraîssant précisément dans la Revue des Deux Mondes, s'adresse à un public qui a un certain raffinement académique, et que les brutalités ou même les simples vivacités pourraient nuire beaucoup au succès de l'œuvre près de ce public spécial; 3) que, littérairement, l'opinion de ce public spécial est de grande importance pour vous, et qu'il serait fort maladroit de ne pas la ménager, 4) enfin que, *dans le volume*, on peut toujours rétablir les passages que l'on regrette. (Arslan, Dame, galline e regine 124)[23]

Clarifying that although certain eliminations were necessary to ensure the novel's appreciation by the journal's elite public, Hérelle suggests the cuts could be remedied later when the novel was published in volume. Although Neera is initially cooperative, later when she is confronted with the draft revealing the elimination of the novel's final chapter, which the French translator failed to appreciate, she refuses to compromise. The omission of *L'indomani*'s final chapter signifies, in fact, the elimination of the scene between Marta and her mother, in which Neera proposes the redemption offered to women by maternity. Regardless of her desire to be published in France in the prestigious *Revue des Deux Mondes*, Neera refuses to allow her novel and her ideas to be manipulated, as her handwritten note dated December 26, 1899, conserved together with the draft of the translation of *L'indomani*, reveals:

Bozze dell'*Indomani* tradotto ridotto e corretto dal signor George [sic!] Hérelle per la *Revue des deux Mondes*. Questo lavoro non venne poi pubblicato perché io, pur riconoscendo la fine traduzione letteraria, trovo la mia idea fondamentale talmente svisata dalla soppressione arbitraria che mi è impossibile accettarlo e firmarlo (Arslan *Dame, galline e regine* 132).[24]

Ten years later, in 1909, the prestigious Italian publisher Treves published an illustrated edition of *L'indomani* with a preface by Neera. In the new preface, she continues to defend her novel and her decision not to bend to Hérellè's judgment, revealing pride in her courage to resist: "Avevo trascurato un'occasione unica, mostrandomi più difficile di un re – Enrico IV aveva ben ceduto a una messa per ottenere Parigi – ma non riuscirono a smuovermi e perdetti Parigi per pochi fogli di stampa. [I had overlooked a unique opportunity, revealing myself more difficult than a king - Henry IV had given in to a mass to obtain Paris - but they could not move me and I lost Paris for a few sheets of print] (L'indomani vii). Although Neera is acutely aware of the opportunity she sacrificed in renouncing Hérellè's offer, she justifies her decision in the new preface to *L'indomani* by establishing the link between a child of the intellect and a child of the flesh:

> il mio primo impulso, senza ombra di esitazione, fu subito di dire di no; ma anche il secondo, anche il terzo, tutti gli impulsi dell'anima mia che avevano concorso a fare dell'*Indomani* un figlio dell'amore, bello di tutto il mio slancio, di tutta la mia giovinezza, di tutta la mia idealità, risposero: no! (L'indomani v)[25]

Just as Marta comes to realize her dignity and redemption as mother, through her experience with *Revue des Deux Mondes*,

Neera realizes and defends the dignity of her role as writer, giving life to and affirming the right to life of her "offspring". With her defense of *L'indomani*, Neera asserts her authority as author, demonstrating in both private and public contexts strength and courage in defending her ideals and the worth of her production.

The Maternal in Neera's Epistolary Exchanges

In other epistolary exchanges, Neera demonstrates a maternal interest in fostering relationships with young male writers and in guiding these new members within literary circles. These correspondences reflect her ideas on women's nurturing nature, expounded not only in novels such as *L'indomani* but also in the context of her theoretical writings, as the following passage from the article "Tutte madri" exemplifies: "La donna che sa educare, che plasma una intelligenza, che sviluppa un'anima, è madre anche se fanciulla; occupa quindi la prima dignità femminile" [The woman who knows how to educate, who moulds an intelligence, who develops a soul, is a mother even if she is a child; she therefore occupies the principal female dignity] (*Le idee di una donna* 864). Neera dedicated an entire volume, titled *Il libro di mio figlio* (My son's book, 1891), to communicating her maternal guidance and offering the counsel derived from her experiences as mother and woman. The book, defined by Neera in the volume's preface as "un dizionario dell'anima" [a dictionary of the soul] and "un catalogo di idee" [a catalog of ideas] is dedicated to her son Adolfo to be used "in tutti i casi dove non sarai ben sicuro di te e dove ti apparirà un aspetto nuovo della vita e degli uomini" [in all the cases where you're not sure of yourself and where a new aspect of life and men will appear to you] (*Il libro di mio figlio* 704). The small pamphlet contains maxims of conduct such as the one that opens the volume: "Qualunque tu voglia essere, o galantuomo e briccone, siilo per intero" [Whatever you want to be, either gallant man or rascal, be it in full] (*Il libro di mio figlio* 705). She advises her son to be honest and virtuous, to do good deeds and to heed his conscience rather than social norms as the judge of his actions. Neera's authority to instruct derives from her life experiences rather than from scholastic formation, as she reveals in another passage from the volume: "L'educazione più potente di tutte ... è la scuola della vita" [The most powerful education of all... is the school of life] (710). The nurturing attitude and tone expressed in *Il libro di mio figlio* foreshadows the motherly role she adopts in epistolary exchanges with young male writers and critics in which she presents her authority as deriving from an expertise in life experiences as well as literary affairs.

In her letter exchanges with literary critic Jakša Čedomil,[26] poet and newspaper director Angiolo Orvieto and crepuscular poet Marino Moretti, all of whom were significantly younger than her,[27] Neera exudes confidence regarding her ability to instruct these young writers on a subject she knows from direct experience: on how to feel and write passionately. Neera's epistolary exchanges with Čedomil, Orvieto and Moretti abound with her suggestions regarding her correspondents' literary and critical styles and exemplify her desire to educate and influence budding writers. While she advises Čedomil to "non attenersi al giudizio degli altri" [disregard others' judgment] (Graciotti 177) in his criticism on Italian literature, her letters to Orvieto and Moretti exhibit both appreciation for and disapproval of their poetic styles. Neera's advice to her correspondents is not limited to advice of a purely professional nature: she adopts a maternal role in counseling her young correspondents on how to feel as a way of instructing them how to write. In such a way, Neera becomes a spiritual as well as poetic guide for her young correspondents.

The correspondence between Neera and Čedomil consists of 15 letters written by Neera between June 15, 1893 and July 30, 1895.[28] Although the correspondence begins rather formally, the content of Neera's letters soon passes from work-related topics to offering advice of a personal nature. On January 13, 1894, she writes:

> Amare, amare, amare, non c'è altra via! Che importa soffrire? … Altre anime conobbi come la sua e sempre mi ispirarono un profondo sentimento di pietà, quasi un bisogno materno di riscaldarle. Se lo scrivermi, se lo sfogo sincero con una persona tanto iniziata alla vita da poterle dir tutto, le fa bene, mi scriva… (Graciotti 182)[29]

Neera presents her authority to advise and guide Čedomil as deriving from her age, but also and primarily from her life experiences and from her awareness that only through feeling and suffering passionately does one truly live and grow spiritually. In a letter dated February 4, 1894, she states, "Ella parla male della passione … pensi che senza di essa nulla di vivo, di bello, di grande sarebbe nel mondo" [You speak badly of passion ... you must realize that without it nothing alive, beautiful, great would exist in the world?] (Graciotti 181). Her letters to Čedomil provide her with an outlet for the expression of her thoughts on an ideal form of love, the platonic kind, which she develops and explores also in her theoretical and narrative works of those years.

Neera's correspondence with Orvieto begins in 1889, with his letter requesting her collaboration with the journal *Vita Nuova.*[30] However, it is only in 1893, when Orvieto sends Neera a copy of his first volume of poetry *La sposa mistica e altri versi* (The mystical bride and other verses), that their epistolary exchange intensifies. In 1893, Neera is already an affirmed novelist and journalist, whereas Orvieto is at the beginning of his career as poet and journalist.[31] Orvieto, who often signs his letters to Neera under the Shakespearian pseudonym Ariele, regards her as a kindred soul who appreciates his poetry and shares his understanding of the misery of modern, bourgeois life, as the following affirmation reveals: "Soffro orribilmente per le miserie pratiche della nostra vita borghese" [I suffer horribly for the practical miseries of our bourgeois life] (Arslan and Zambon 81). Neera responds by encouraging him to "rivolgersi a [lei] nei momenti tristi" [turn to her in difficult moments] (Arlsan and Zambon 84) and to dedicate himself to his work. When he writes her in April 1893 that "c'è chi vive troppo presto ed io, purtroppo, sono di questi" [there are those who live too soon and I, unfortunately, am one of them] (Arslan and Zambon 75), Neera responds by encouraging the young poet to follow her example: "Non le dirò quanti anni ho più di lei, ma son parecchi purtroppo, eppure non mi sento finita. … Ho una sete di bello, di alto, di puro, che quando giungo a soddisfare mi dà ebbrezze inaudite" [I won't tell you how much older I am than you, but a lot, unfortunately, and yet I don't feel finished. ... I have a thirst for beauty, for heights, for purity, which when I manage to satisfy it, it gives me unprecedented euphoria] (Arslan and Zambon 79).

Neera's authority as guide for Orvieto resides in her experience not only as a woman who shares common ideas on the nature of love but also as a writer. Neera advises Orvieto on his poetic style, emphasizing the importance of content over form in the expression of passion and emotion in a letter dated November 16, 1896:

> L'arte è figlia primogenita di Amore. Si potrà avere qualche lieve controversia sulla ricerca della madre, Psiche o Venere, ma Amore è il padre legittimo dell'arte. Dove l'amore manca l'arte è fredda, povera, decadente – arte di bimbi immaturi o di

> vecchi esauriti. Vi parla una donna, caro amico, che di queste cose unicamente visse! (Arlsan and Zambon 186)[32]

Neera's epistolary exchange with Angiolo Orvieto reveals a shared understanding of art as anti-naturalistic and aristocratic.[33] In a letter to Orvieto dated April 15, 1893, Neera writes regarding her latest novel *Nel sogno* that it is "un inno all'idealismo" [a hymn to idealism] (Arslan and Zambon 79). Orvieto's letters to Neera confirm that he views her as both a poetic and spiritual guide, a writer whose work reflects her ideas on the supremacy of spiritual over physical love, as he reveals in a letter dated September 26, 1894, in which he addresses her as "una nobile anima, alata e sognatrice, appassionata ed onesta, assetata di cose nuove ed arcane," [a noble soul, winged and dreamy, passionate and honest, thirsty for new and arcane things] (Arslan and Zambon 152).

Neera's epistolary exchange with another young poet, Marino Moretti, reveals her continued faith in her ideal of content over form.[34] In a letter to Moretti dated March 27, 1911, Neera advises Moretti: "Bisogna amare profondamente, e profondamente pensare, e soffrire e godere nell'intimo delle nostre fibre; e voltare e rivoltare queste nostre sofferenze, queste nostre gioie, questi nostri pensieri dentro di noi finché siano diventati sangue del nostro sangue. Allora si scrive! Non prima" [It is necessary to love deeply, and to think deeply, and to suffer and enjoy in the depths of our fibers; and to go over and over within us these sufferings, these joys, these thoughts until they have become blood of our blood. Then one writes! Not before] (Zambon and Pegoraro 79). Neera's epistolary exchange with Moretti spans from 1910 to 1914, and regardless of the differences between the two writers' styles and poetics,[35] their exchange reveals that Neera views in Moretti a young mind to be shaped as well as his acceptance of her guidance. In a letter dated October 27, 1910, Neera writes, "Mi interessai a lei come ad un continuatore delle battaglie che combattei io stessa" [I took an interest in you as a continuer of the battles I fought myself] (Zambon and Pegoraro 48). Neera views Moretti as a son in art capable of continuing her struggle to assert her artistic ideals. He accepts Neera's role as spiritual and poetic guide, stating in a letter on November 13, 1910: "Grazie ancora, cara signora, del bene che le Sue pagine mi hanno fatto. Grazie della bella cartolina in cui ò ravvisato con gioia l'illustre e cara amica, la maestra di idealità, il poeta della passione" [Thank you again, dear lady, for the good your pages have done me. Thank you for the beautiful postcard in which I saw with joy the illustrious and dear friend, the teacher of idealism, the poet of passion] (Zambon and Pegoraro 54). Needy of Neera's approval, Moretti defends the realism of his poetry against Neera's criticism of it as "fotografia di cattivo gusto" [photograph in bad taste] when he writes in a letter dated October 28, 1910: "Oh, non mi faccia il torto di credermi un materialista! … Io sono uno *spiritualista*, creda: ma ò bisogno di tenermi alla terra per scrivere" [Oh, don't make the mistake of thinking I'm a materialist! ... I'm a spiritualist, believe me, but I need to keep myself tied to the earth to write] (Zambon and Pegoraro 49).

For Neera, the expression of one's spirit is intimately linked to poetic expression and Moretti's failure to "open" the window to his soul accounts for Neera's negative appraisal of his poetry, as she confirms in a letter dated September 2, 1910, regarding Moretti's *I lestofanti* (The swindlers): "Certo li loderei con maggior piacere se i soggetti presi a trattare fossero più simpatici o se ella vi avesse lasciato penetrare un po' della sua anima" [Surely I would praise them with greater pleasure if the subjects chosen were more sympathetic or if you had let some of your soul penetrate] (Zambon and Pegoraro 43). The divergence of poetic and artistic styles ultimately leads to the end of their correspondence, the reasons for which Neera brusquely announces in a letter dated September 5, 1913: "La colpa è mia, o meglio la disgrazia, ma mi è insopportabile trattenere per forza una corrispondenza che non trova più in se stessa la propria ragione di vita. … Che cosa vi dovrei dire? Nulla voi avete da dire a me; il vostro cuore, la vostra anima mi sono rimasti chiusi" [The fault is mine, or rather the misfortune, but it is unbearable for me to carry on a correspondence that no longer finds in itself its reason for existing. What should I say to you? You have nothing to say to me; your heart and soul are closed to me] (Zambon and Pegoraro 186). Neera reveals that her role as poetic guide is closely tied to the communion of spirits with her correspondent. Moretti responds to Neera's farewell by defending what Neera refers to as his "sentimental aridity" as a fundamental aspect of his poetic personality:

> Le mie poesie, lo sapete, sono piene di grigio. Ebbene, quel grigio non era, non è una posa. Io sono un povero essere ammalato – come potrebbe dire una poetessa moderna - di aridità sentimentale. … Io quando vi vidi per la prima volta sentii di accostarmi a uno spirito alto e puro e m'infervorai come mi son sempre infervorato quando sono stato con voi nel parlatorio,

> e cioè vi ho voluto bene, vi ho ammirata, vi ho sentita superiore a me, sempre, come cuore e come artista. (Zambon and Pegoraro 187)[36]

Regardless of the differences in poetics between the two writers, Moretti continues to revere Neera as a spiritual and poetic guide.

Understanding and Solidarity between Women Writers

Neera maintained correspondences with women writers, such as journalist and novelist Matilde Serao and poets Vittoria Aganoor and Ada Negri, with whom she adopted the role of neither mother nor daughter but instead that of a sister. The letters Neera received from these women writers provide the basis for an understanding of the network of collaboration that existed between women writers of the period. Whereas budding writers such as Negri and Aganoor address Neera in their letters with admiration and respect for her production and the success she had achieved in male-dominated literary circles, the letters from affirmed writer Serao reveal the willingness of one woman writer to help another. The private and intimate nature of the epistolary exchange offered women writers the setting to openly express their support and respect for each other.

Neera's archive features two letters from Ada Negri, the first of which is dated May 20, 1892, the year of publication of Neera's novel *Senio* and Negri's volume of poetry *Fatalità* (Fate). In this letter, Negri writes:

> Senio mi ha lasciata una impressione profonda. Non ho mai letto alcuna opera di donna che s'avvicini a tanta grandezza e lucidità d'ideali. Ciò che mi avvince è la calma robusta e immensa dello stile che è tutto un getto, senza uno sforzo, senza declamazione, senza una debolezza – vera assimilazione, se così si può dire, del pensiero alla forma. Sono molto ignorante della scienza e della vita: solo una strana e ardentissima potenza d'intuizione mi guida in arte come in tutto. … Io la ringrazio, Signora, di avermi procurato colla lettura del suo libro sensazioni così vibranti. (Arslan, Dame, galline e regine 203)[37]

Negri identifies Neera as a woman writer who has achieved literary greatness in the stylistic form of her production, recognizing in Neera's intuitive and spontaneous mode of expression a model for her own way of writing. She "confesses" to Neera her lack of knowledge, at least that deriving from formal studies and from experience, revealing instead how she finds inspiration for her writing in another, more intimate source: intuition. It is interesting to note that Negri exalts qualities of Neera's work, such as its direct and straightforward nature, that were often noted as defects of women writers' works by male literary critics because they were seen to denote a lack of formal training. Neera served as a model for other women writers not only for the success she achieved with the public and critics but for the intimate stylistic quality of her production.

The correspondence between Neera and Aganoor dates from December 1896 to January 1910, the year of Aganoor's death. In 1896, Neera is already an affirmed writer, whereas Aganoor would not publish her first volume of poetry, *Leggenda eterna* (Eternal legend), until 1900. The exchange begins rather formally, with Aganoor addressing Neera as *Signora* and adopting the formal *Lei*, passing, however, in the seventh letter dated September 1900 to the informal and intimate *tu* and use of Neera's first name Anna. Regardless of the formality of the initial letters, Aganoor's tone is already intimate from her first letter: "sento in Lei un'amica, e confido che m'ascolti con indulgenza" [I feel I have a friend in you, and I trust you will listen to me with indulgence] (Arslan, "Un'amicizia tra letterate" 48). Aganoor addresses Neera in her letters not only as friend but with terms such as "anima fraterna" [fraternal soul], "sorella" [sister], "poeta" [poet], "anima d'artista" [artistic soul] and "collega in scrittura" [colleague in writing], revealing the bond between the two correspondents as not only one of friendship but one of respect between two colleagues. Aganoor reveals her admiration for Neera as one of few women writers, if not the only one, who has succeeded in the literary profession, writing in a letter dated August 11, 1903: "E tu sei l'*unica* scrittrice, vivente, di romanzi, che scriva veramente *il puro italiano*, senza leziosaggini e senza sciatterie, *squisitamente* insomma" [And you're the only living novelist who really writes pure Italian, without laziness and sloppiness, in conclusion exquisitely] (Arslan, "Un'amicizia tra letterate" 62). While she praises Neera's linguistic style, Aganoor indirectly expresses her opinion of the general state of women writers' literary production, recognizing the defects in style and language that were often noted in women writers' works. In another passage, Aganoor reveals how she, as woman writer, participates in Neera's success: "È inutile ch'io Le dica come io L'abbia sempre seguita nel suo cammino trionfale con ammirazione *orgogliosa*; *orgogliosa* sì, perché appunto io sentivo spesso nella mia anima vibrare fraternamente la sua voce, quella dell'anima sua, e questa affinità m'inorgogliva" [It is useless for me to tell you how I have always followed you on your triumphal journey with proud admiration; proud, yes, because I often heard your voice, that of your soul, vibrate fraternally in my soul, and this affinity made me proud] (Arslan, "Un'amicizia tra letterate" 49). Aganoor rejoices in Neera's ability to express a female voice in which she and other women proudly recognize their own internal voices. In a letter dated March 19, 1907, Aganoor further reveals her understanding of Neera as capable of expressing the female "*anima*" [soul], in contrast to the empty male voice of patriarchal society:

> Ti dirò solo che ier l'altro fui a pranzo al Quirinale e mentre si facevano quei soliti discorsi *sciapiti*, (parole, o piuttosto ombre di parole, vuote di pensiero e talora anche di *senso*, somiglianti a certe orrendissime *frutta di bambage,* che fanno le monache nei conventi, e che a premere un poco, *cedono*, e non ne resta che un cencio) pensavo con indicibile desiderio a te, cara e alta amica mia e devi aver *sentito* il mio saluto venirti dietro. (Arslan, "Un'amicizia tra letterate" 67–68)[38]

Neera's work represents for Aganoor an example of a different kind of expression, in contrast to the shallowness she associates with the male voice of patriarchal discourse.

In a letter dated September 17, 1900, Aganoor refers to Neera's female readers and admirers as part of an invitation to visit her home: "mia sorella Elena vuole che ti ripeta che avresti qua libertà *piena* e delle antiche ammiratrici ad accoglierti, delle leggitrici non volgari delle tue opere, che ti amarono anche prima di conoscerti, e si augurarono di poter stringere un giorno quella tua nobile mano valorosa" [my sister Elena wants me to tell you once again that you would have full freedom here and old admirers to welcome you, non vulgar readers of your works, who loved you even before they met you, and wished they could one day shake that noble and valiant hand of yours] (Arslan, "Un'amicizia tra letterate" 54). Aganoor praises Neera for having established a model of female literary success for women of her generation but also for women of later generations: "Quanto e come è poeta lei! . . . Come sarà orgogliosa sua figlia d'avere una mammina quale è lei! Scrive anch'essa?" [How poetic you are! ... How proud your daughter will be to have a mommy like you! Does she write too?] (Arslan, "Un'amicizia tra letterate" 51).

In the transmission from mother to daughter and from woman to woman of a positive female model, Aganoor recognizes Neera as the beginner of a female literary lineage.

Aganoor's letters to Neera reveal the sharing between two women writers of the experiences and difficulties encountered within the literary profession. To achieve literary success, Aganoor suggests, the woman writer battles the "stupida critica moderna" [stupid modern criticism] (Arslan "Un'amicizia tra letterate" 62), which fails to find the true meaning of one's production often because critics do not even read the works they review (Arslan "Un'amicizia tra letterate" 62). Regardless of the difficulties encountered, Aganoor considers writing more than a profession, referring to it as a need: "Ma lo scrivere, tu lo sai bene, è un *bisogno*, e quando siamo intesi al nostro lavoro (ciascuno secondo le proprie forze) tale è l'obblìo del pubblico, dei suoi giudizi, delle miserie delle gare, del plauso mondano, che ci manchi pure a cose fatte l'approvazione e la lode" [But writing, you know well, is a need, and when we are focused on our work (each according to one's own strength), such is the neglect of the public, of its judgments, of the miseries of the competition, of the worldly praise, that we also lack even the approval and praise of things done] (Arslan "Un'amicizia tra letterate" 62). Recalling the abundant negative critical reception that women writers often received from male critics, discussed earlier in this study, it is interesting to note, as Mitchell points out in *Italian Women Writers: Gender and Everyday Life in Fiction and Journalism*, that "[f]emale-authored reviews of writings by women were, more often than not, very positive" (110) and that "[i]t is quite likely that such displays of deference on behalf of female critics towards women writers contributed in no small measure to women writers' growing sense of self-confidence and self-esteem in the public eye" (110).

Even in the letter exchange between Neera and Serao, whose shared status as two of the leading women writers of late nineteenth-century Italy provided a possible motive for competition, it is possible to observe an openness and willingness to aid another woman writer. The 15 letters written by Serao in Neera's archive reveal the Neapolitan writer's close attention, which we can presume to have been reciprocated,[39] to following Neera's activity as a writer. In a letter dated December 2, 1881, Serao writes: "Del resto io mi occupo sempre di voi, leggendovi ansiosamente dove scrivete. … Così, tra le linee studio il vostro pensiero e la vostra vita" [After all, I always follow you, anxiously reading where you write. ... So between the lines I study your thoughts and your life] (Collino Pansa,

"Una femminista d'altri tempi" 173). Serao, like Aganoor, reveals the woman writer's ability to "read between the lines" of another woman writer's production. In the letter dated December 31, 1885, Serao writes, "lo sapete che vi voglio bene assai, come dicono a Napoli: e quando ricevo una lettera vostra, in mezzo a tante noie, ho una buona consolazione. Ho pochissime amiche, ma su voi conto e a voi punto, cara e simpatica, molto spesso, anche lavorando" [You know that I love you very much, as they say in Naples: and when I receive a letter from you, in the midst of so much trouble, I have a good consolation. I have very few friends, but I am counting on you, and I am going to strive to reach you, who are dear and nice, very often, even while working] (Trotta 96). Serao, established and affirmed writer and journalist, acknowledges in the private context afforded by the epistolary genre the importance of a female point of reference, on both personal and professional levels, within the male-dominated literary circles of the day.

In 1920, Serao led the commemoration ceremony in memory of Neera, recognizing in her speech, later published as *Ricordando Neera,* Neera's dedication to women's issues and crediting Neera with promoting her own feminist program: "Ella, anzi, con il suo bel valore, affrontò tutte le questioni che sommovevano l'irrequieto mondo muliebre e le discusse serenamente ma con ardore e da tutto il confusissimo programma femminista, cercò trarre quanto poteva essere sorgente di vera elevazione sociale della donna" [She, indeed, with her magnificent worth, tackled all the issues that agitate the restless female world and discussed them serenely but ardently and from all the confused feminist program, she tried to extract what could be a source of true social elevation for women] (39). In referring to Neera as "la mia sorella in arte" [my sister in art] (24) and "l'apostolo della vita spirituale" [the apostle of spiritual life] (37), Serao reveals a communion of spirits based on their shared identity as women writers as well as a profound respect for Neera's literary ideal. Serao's reference to Neera as her *sorella in arte* reveals, as Mitchell notes, "the sense of *sorellanza* which bound the relatively small number of middle-class women entering the male-dominated public sphere in the late nineteenth century in Italy [which] cut across divisions of social class, differences of opinion on the 'woman question', and regional boundaries" (200).

Neera's attention toward creating a female network was not only limited to epistolary exchanges. Literary endeavors such as the volume *Dizionario d'igiene per le famiglie* (Dictionary of hygiene for families, 1881),[40] a sort of conduct manual "specialmente scritto per le donne e per le famiglie" [written especially for women and for families] (Neera, *Dizionario* 1–2), and the women's literary journal *Vita Intima*, founded and directed by Neera together with a group of female intellectuals in Milan in 1890,[41] are further testimony of her goal of addressing issues that directly concerned women. The entries in *Dizionario d'igiene per le famiglie* instruct women on a range of issues, from those of a strictly female nature, such as breastfeeding, to advice regarding daily habits, such as coffee consumption, and the analysis of conditions such as *nevrosismo* [nervousness], guiding the volume's readers on how to cope with the challenges that come with adapting to the changes of the modern era. Neera's dictionary entry on "casa" [home] reveals how the changes taking place within society led to a certain amount of newfound freedom for women who no longer found their sphere of activity limited to the home:

> Finché la donna si è accontentata dei suoi attributi naturali, la casa bastava all'impiego della sua attività; ora le donne si annoiano a stare in casa, perché vanno sempre più perdendo la loro caratteristica femminile, ed alle placide soste sul verone, alla conversazione, ai lavoretti d'ago, preferiscono gli svaghi rumorosi della piazza e le passeggiate meccaniche in su e in giù del Corso. (Dizionario 97–98)[42]

In *Vita Intima,* women and issues directly concerning them were also front and center also in Vita Intima, as illustrated by an editorial from the journal's first issue:

> Per Te, che leggi. *Vita Intima* ti saluta, graziosa lettrice. ... Gli uomini hanno i loro giornali che leggono per le vie, nei caffè, nei clubs, nei teatri, un po' dappertutto e in ogni tempo; ... O perché non potrai avere anche tu il *tuo* giornale; il giornale che viva la tua *vita intima*, e con una visita settimanale ti porti l'eco del mormorio confuso della grande onda femminile: riveli a te stessa l'anima tua, s'occupi della tua persona, della tua casa, di ciò che ami, e forma quasi l'intimo tessuto della tua esistenza, del piccolo mondo dove incontrastata regni ed imperi? (Arslan, "Un progetto culturale temerario e il suo fallimento: 'Vita Intima' (1891–92)", 211)[43]

With this dedication, Neera's journal offered its female audience a window onto the changing society of the time, proposing itself as a filter for understanding and interpreting transformations, particularly those brought about by the *onda femminile* of the women's emancipation movement. As Arslan observes in "Un progetto culturale temerario e il suo fallimento: 'Vita Intima' (1891–92)":

> Come non vedere qui il proposito, così fermo in Neera, di aiutare le donne a riflettere sulla loro propria via alla conoscenza di sé, alla comprensione della propria originalità di intelletto e di sentimento, perché tutte trovino la loro strada e imparino a opporsi all'oppressione cieca di costumi antiquati, di paternalismi repressivi, di zitellaggi senza speranza? (213–214)[44]

These projects together with Neera's letter exchanges offer an inside view onto the public and private voices of this woman writer and the multi-faceted ways in which she positioned herself within fin-de-siècle literary and journalistic circles. The personal and confidential nature of the epistolary correspondence freed Neera from her public persona and the expectations surrounding it. The multiple stances, from daughter to mother to sister, adopted by Neera in her various epistolary relationships reveal not only the complexity of operating within the male-dominated environments of her time but also, more importantly, Neera's ability to navigate them successfully.

Notes

1 For an overview of the nature of Neera's archive, see Arslan, "L'archivio privato di Neera" and Arlslan and Pasqui 31–45.

2 A single letter or note has been found from Salvatore Di Giacomo, Luigi Gualdo, Giovanni Cena, Gabriele D'Annunzio and Edoardo De Amicis.

3 What emerges from these correspondences is a secret Neera that integrates and completes the somewhat reticent and contradictory image that can be drawn from her published works, where, in years sometimes very close to each other, she alternated between positions and statements of a character that today would be decidedly "reactionary" and other subtly courageous and - for that period - also daring, or frankly naturalistic novels, such as *Teresa*, and others with an exasperatingly idealistic imprint, such as *Nel sogno*.

4 A most interesting literary branch is that which collects the Epistolaries, even though private letters are not really part of literature, since the letter is generally not a manifestation of study and doctrine but the simple fulfillment of a social function. Neera. "Lettere." *Il Marzocco*, vol. XVI, no. 36, 9 Mar., 1911.

5 Letter to Marino Moretti dated December 20, 1910. See Zambon and Pegoraro 57.

6 Gustavo Botta (1880–1948) was a Milanese poet and literary and art critic. Martini notes that Botta "fu un eccellente intenditore d'arte e di letteratura, specialmente francese" (195–196).

7 Giuseppe Saverio Gargàno (1859–1930) was a Neapolitan literary critic and journalist who collaborated with literary journals such as *Vita Nuova*, *Nazione Letteraria* and *Il Marzocco.*

8 I also want to tell you that in all this time we haven't seen each other I have thought about you and precisely every time I was struggling with the new novel that has been languishing for several months on my desk, paralyzed by a singular slowness of execution. I've become difficult and I also struggle strenuously, in my own small way, in the search for the word - not refined but exact.

9 I feel this need to speak at certain times a different, wider, more harmonious language, which has the lightness of flight and the sound of an echo, which palpitates like a wing and groans like a spring and flashes with a thousand iridescences like a ray of sunshine through a drop of dew.

10 I don't [uderstand] anything about poetry, I don't know the metrics, I am a perfect ignoramus; though I don't know why in certain rare moments of life those short lines flow from my heart full of my tears and dreams. I would like to know if there is anything in them worth keeping. I am, I repeat, so incompetent in the matter that it is impossible to judge for myself.

11 Emanuele Navarro della Miraglia (1838–1919), journalist and author of short stories and novels such as *Storielle siciliane* and *La nana*, was active in Sicilian *verist* literary circles in the years 1870–90.

12 Navarro, from Rome, made me finalize a contract with Sommaruga for the publication of one of my novels for next Christmas. This was four days ago. In these four days, as if on purpose, I am receiving alarming and dishonorable news from all sides regarding Sommaruga and those who write with him. I live so out of this world, and I am so unfamiliar with its intricacies, that I find myself embarrassed. ... You must know these things. Tell me one word- do I break it or not? Although Neera's novel *Il marito dell'amica* was published, and paid for, by Sommaruga in the journal *Nabab* from December 1884 to February 1885, financial ruin forced the editor to emigrate a mere few months later.

13 In the letter to Gargàno, Neera refers to a May 3, 1903, anonymous review of *Una passione* in *Fanfulla della domenica.*

14 You feel alone, alone with [your book], with your dream, with your illusion, with your passion; alone in the big world that doesn't look at you, that doesn't care at all about what you have written for it, that doesn't care at all about your thoughts and beliefs; that works, eats, sleeps, goes for a walk, has fun, is bored, is well, is sick, far, far from you and your fantasies. And you look on dazed and grumpy at the shop window where your book lies in the tragic stillness of the dead.

15 I can't explain the tone that, if it didn't belong to a lovely lady, I would call almost rude with which you answered yesterday to my exhortations to continue and finish the series of your wedding sketches. I don't think I ever disrespected you, a learned and kind lady, nor do I think the newspaper ever disrespected you. I am unaware whether the

administration, in these months of frequent absences and increased duties, and summer slowness, delayed any payment to you - but I know that your account is completely settled - so the delay can only have been brief.

16 I'm not surprised that they haven't published some of your writings; they won't have understood it; they don't know what value the other writings you has published have. They disrespect a woman and an artist. I say these things in confidence, taking this opportunity to express my admiration for you.

17 Angiolo Orvieto. "*L'Indomani.*" *Vita Nuova*, vol. I, p. 37.

18 When your article on *Vita Nuova* came out, I was already sick; but if there was regret (neither anger nor revenge), it was regarding only the neglect afforded my book, while the *Vita* that is called *New* and that should be *Italian*, dedicated long columns to novelists from the other side of the Alps... It is always so here with us. They beat us, and we lick them!

19 Roberto Bracco (1861–1943) was a Neapolitan playwright, poet, writer and journalist. His correspondence with Neera is examined in Saladino.

20 Saladino notes that the date indicated on the letter, 27/10/80, is incorrect for the references to a preceding letter dated November 14, 1891. Saladino suggests December 27, 1891, as the correct date.

21 Vittorio Pica (1864–1930), Neapolitan journalist and literary critic, is recognized for his role in introducing and disseminating French symbolism in Italian literary circles. Neera and Pica's epistolary exchange has been published in Finotti.

22 For translations, one should not think about France: Verga and Fogazzaro did not have any success there and if D'Annunzio was liked, it was due not only to his exceptional artistic value, but also and above all to his subtle, refined, and somewhat morbid psychology in accordance with the most recent exquisite trends in young literature from beyond the Alps.

23 Think about it: 1) that the readers of Revue are not ordinary readers ... 2) that your book, appearing precisely in the Revue des Deux Mondes, is addressed to an audience that has a certain academic refinement, and that brutalities or even simple vivacities could be very detrimental to the success of the work with this special audience; 3) that, literarily, the opinion of this special public is of great importance to you, and that it would be very awkward not to spare it, 4) finally that, in the volume, one can always restore the passages that one wishes restored.

24 Drafts of *Indomani* translated edited and corrected by Mr. George [sic!] Hérelle for the *Revue des deux Mondes*. This work was not published because I, while recognizing the fine literary translation, find my fundamental idea so distorted by the arbitrary suppression that it is impossible for me to accept and sign it.

25 My first impulse, without a shadow of hesitation, was immediately to say no; but even the second, even the third, all the impulses of my soul that had contributed to making *L'Indomani* a child of love, beautiful from all my impetus, all my youth, all my idealism, they all replied: no!

26 Jakša Čedomil is the literary pseudonym of Jakov Cuka (1868–1929). Graciotti notes that Čedomil is considered "l'iniziatore in Croazia

di una critica di misura europea" and credited with "il merito di far conoscere in Croazia la letteratura italiana e in Italia le letterature serbo-croata e russa" (175).

27 Neera and Čedomil's exchange lasts from 1893 to 1895. At its start, Neera was 47 and Čedomil 24. Neera and Orvieto's exchange lasts from 1889, when Neera was 43 and Orvieto 20, to 1917. Neera and Moretti correspond from 1910, when she was 64 and he 25, until 1914.

28 Neera did not keep Čedomil's letters. The *carteggio* has been published in Graciotti.

29 Love, love, love, there's no other way! Who cares to suffer? ... I knew other souls like yours and they always inspired me with a deep feeling of pity, almost a maternal need to warm them. If writing to me, if sincere expression with a person so initiated in life to tell you anything, is good for you, write to me.

30 *Vita Nuova* was a literary, artistic and philosophical periodical published weekly from January 20, 1889, to January 1891, and then monthly until March 1891 under the direction of Orvieto, Giuseppe Saverio Gargàno, Diego Garoglio and Giuseppe Andrea Fabris.

31 Throughout his career, Orvieto collaborated with the journals *Vita Nuova, Nazione Letteraria* and *Il Marzocco.*

32 Art is Love's firstborn daughter. There may be some slight controversy about the search for the mother, Psyche or Venus, but Love is the legitimate father of art. Where love is missing art is cold, poor, decadent – art of immature children or exhausted old men. Speaking to you is a woma, dear friend, who lived exclusively of these matters!

33 Neera and Orvieto's *carteggio* has been published in Arslan and Zambon.

34 Neera and Moretti's exchange has been published in the Zambon and Pegoraro.

35 Moretti is one of the exponents of the crepuscular poetic movement, a poetic style that Neera completely fails to appreciate as her comments regarding Moretti's poetry reveal.

36 My poems, you know, are full of gray. Well, that gray was not, is not a pose. I am a poor being sick – as a modern poetess might say – from sentimental dryness. ... When I saw you for the first time I felt that I was approaching a high and pure spirit and I became as enraged as I have always been when I was with you in the parlor, and that is, I loved you, I admired you, I felt you superior to me, always, as a heart and as an artist.

37 *Senio* made a deep impression on me. I have never read any woman's work that comes close to such greatness and clarity of ideals. What fascinates me is the robust and immense calmness of the style that is all a jet, without effort, without declamation, without a weakness - true assimilation, if one can say so, of thought to form. I am very ignorant of science and life: only a strange and ardent power of intuition guides me in art as in everything. ... I thank you, Madam, for having provided me with such vibrant sensations from reading your book.

38 I will tell you only that yesterday I was at lunch at the Quirinale and while we were making those usual *dull* speeches, (words, or rather shadows of words, empty of thought and sometimes even of *meaning*,

resembling some horrible *cotton fruits*, which nuns make in convents, and that to press a little, they *yield*, and there is nothing left but a rag) I thought with unspeakable desire of you, my dear and high friend, and you must have *felt* my greeting coming after you.

39 Arslan notes that "le lettere sono senza riscontri e costituiscono solo una parte di uno scambio che dovette essere molto più fitto." See Trotta 95.

40 The volume was written in collaboration with Paolo Mantegazza.

41 The journal ran weekly from June 1890 to December 1891, featuring articles by various writers, male and female, from all areas of Italy, such as Marchesa Colombi, Roberto Bracco, Federico De Roberto, Anna Vertua Gentile, Ines Benaglio Castellani Fantoni and Matilde Serao.

42 As long as woman was satisfied with her natural attributes, the house was enough for carrying out her activity; now women are bored to stay at home, because they are losing more and more their feminine characteristics, and they prefer the noisy amusements of the square and the mechanical walks up and down the Corso to the tranquil time spent on the balcony, to conversation, to needlework.

43 For you, who reads. *Vita Intima* greets you, pretty reader. ... Men have their newspapers that they read in the streets, in cafes, clubs, theatres, everywhere and at all times; ... Now why can't you have *your* newspaper too; the newspaper that lives your *intimate life*, and with a weekly visit brings you the echo of the confused murmur of the great feminine wave: that reveals your soul to yourself, takes care of your person, your home, what you love, and forms almost the intimate fabric of your existence, of the small world where you reign and command undisputed?

44 How can we fail to see here the purpose, so firm in Neera, of helping women to reflect on their own way to self-knowledge, to understand their own originality of intellect and feeling, so that they all find their own way and learn to oppose the blind oppression of antiquated customs, of repressive paternalisms, of hopeless spinsters?

References

Arslan, Antonia. *Dame, galline e regine. La scrittura femminile italiana fra '800 e '900*, edited by Marina Pasqui, Milano, Guerini, 1998.

———. "L'archivio inedito della corrispondenza di Neera." *La correspondence (Edition, fonctions, signification).* Aix-en-Provence, Centre aixois de recherches italiennes, 1984, pp. 217–226.

———. "Luigi Capuana e Neera: Corrispondenza inedita 1881–1885." *Miscellanea di studi in onore di Vittore Branca.* Florence, Olschki, 1983, pp. 161–185.

———. "Marinetti e Neera: un curioso scambio di lettere." *Forum Italicum*, vol. 16, 1982, pp. 113–118.

———. "Neera e il giornalismo napoletano: corrispondenze inedite con Roberto Bracco, Federigo Verdinois e Martin Cafiero." *Cultura meridionale e letteratura italiana. I modelli narrativi dell'età moderna. Atti dell'XI Congresso AISLLI. 14–18 aprile 1982*, edited by Pompeo Giannantonio, Naples, Loffredo, 1985, pp. 589–599.

———. "Un'amicizia tra letterate: Vittoria Aganoor e Neera." *Quaderni veneti*, vol. 5, no. 8, 1988, pp. 35–74.

———. "Un progetto culturale temerario e il suo fallimento: 'Vita Intima' (1891–92)." *Donne e giornalismo: Percorsi e presenze di una storia di genere*, edited by Silvia Franchini and Simonetta Soldani, Milan, Franco Angeli, 2004, pp. 211–224.

——— and Anna Folli, editors. *Il concetto che ne informa. Benedetto Croce e Neera. Corrispondenza (1903–1917)*. Naples, Edizioni Scientifiche Italiane, 1988.

——— and Marina Pasqui, editors. *Ritratto di signora. Neera (Anna Radius Zuccari) e il suo tempo*. Milano, Guerini, 1999.

——— and Patrizia Zambon, editors. *Il sogno aristocratico. Angiolo Orvieto e Neera. Corrispondenza 1889–1917*. Milano, Guerini, 1990.

——— and Rita Verdirame. "Giovanni Verga e Neera: un carteggio." *Quaderni di filologia e letteratura siciliana*, vol. 5, 1978, pp. 27–42.

Brotto, Manuela. "Un'artista e lo specchio della critica. Il carteggio inedito tra Neera e Gargàno." *Cuadernos de Filologia Italiana*, vol. 8, 2001, pp. 165–183.

Collino Pansa, Raimondo. "Piccolo viaggio in un archivio. Lettere a Neera." *La Martinella di Milano* vol. 31, 1977, pp. 253–262.

———. "Una femminista d'altri tempi: Neera. Lettere inedite di Matilde Serao, Eleonora Duse e Giacomo Puccini a Neera." *La Martinella di Milano*, vol. 31, 1977, pp. 71–76.

Cousineau, Diane. *Letters and Labyrinths: Women Writing/Cultural Codes*. Newark, U of Delaware P, 1997.

Finotti, Fabio, editor. *Il sistema letterario e diffusione del decadentismo nell'Italia di fine Ottocento. Carteggio Vittorio Pica – Neera*. Firenze, Olschki, 1988.

Graciotti, Sante. "Neera nella corrispondenza inedita con Jakša Čedomil." *Studi sulla cultura lombarda in memoria di Mario Apollonio*. Vol. 2, Milano, Vita e Pensiero, 1971, pp. 172–185.

Martini, Carlo. "Neera e Gustavo Botta." *Nuova antologia*, vol. 2C, 1963, pp. 195–206.

Mitchell, Katharine. *Italian Women Writers: Gender and Everyday Life in Fiction and Journalism, 1870–1910*. Toronto, U of Toronto P, 2014.

Neera. *Dizionario d'igiene per le famiglie*, edited by Maria Corti, Milano, Scheiwiller, 1985.

———. *Il canzoniere della nonna*. 1908. Milano, L.F. Cogliati, 1908.

——— *Il libro di mio figlio*. 1891. *Neera*, edited by Croce, Milan, Garzanti, 1942, pp. 701–749.

———. *L'indomani*. Milan, Treves, 1909.

———. *Le idee di una donna*. 1903. *Neera*, edited by Croce, Milan, Garzanti, 1942, pp. 777–867.

Romani, Gabriella. *Postal Culture: Writing and Reading Letters in Post-Unification Italy*. Toronto, U of Toronto P, 2013.

Saladino, Paola. La riscoperta di una scrittrice: Neera. Con un'appendice di ventiquattro lettere inedite di Roberto Bracco a Neera. 1977–78. Università di Padova, PhD. Dissertation.

Serao, Matilde. *Ricordando Neera.* Milano, Treves, 1920.

Vecchi, Alberto et al. *Metodologia ecdotica dei carteggi. Atti del Convegno Internazionale di Studi Roma 23, 24, 25 ottobre 1980*, edited by Elio d'Auria, Firenze, Monnier, 1989.

Zambon, Patrizia. "Riviste Fiorentine e Milanesi dell'ultimo Ottocento nel carteggio Angiolo Orvieto-Neera." *Il sogno aristocratico.* Angiolo Orvieto e Neera. Corrispondenza 1189–1917, edited by Antonia Arslan and Patrizia Zambon, Milano, Guerini, 1990, pp. 25–44.

——— and Carola Pegoraro, editors. *Neera. Marino Moretti. Il sogno borghese. Corrispondenza 1910–1914.* Milano, Guerini, 1996.

Conclusion

The following affirmation by late nineteenth-century Italian feminist Anna Maria Mozzoni in *La donna e i suoi rapporti sociali* confirms the devastatingly restrictive and oppressive social customs and attitudes faced by women of the period, whether they were writers, housewives, mothers, sisters or daughters:

> Tu non sei capace di lunghi e severi studi, le disse lo scienziato, e le dimostra come due e due fa quattro, che la conformazione del suo cervello, la delicatezza dei suoi tessuti, la debolezza della sua fibra, la molteplicità dei suoi bisogni, la dimostrano irrecusabilmente non nata alla scienza... Lascia ad una bocca meno piccola della tua la difficile articolazione di barbari paroloni, e non voler annuvolare il liscio marmo della tua fronte colle rughe dei calcoli, né voler vedere il tuo celeste sorriso fra le gravi meditazioni, né impallidir le rose del viso tra le veglie prolungate. ... Esclusa dal sapere, la donna, rimaneva esclusa eziandio dal potere; ed eccola ridotta a passività assoluta, cosa e non essere, di maggiore o minor valore relativo, di nessun valore intrinseco, orba d'ogni coscienza di sé che è la prima ragione d'ogni forza. (qtd. Pieroni Bortolotti 39–40)[1]

Regardless of the difficulties facing women in late nineteenth-century Italy, often hindering them from adopting roles outside the home, the last decades of the nineteenth century witnessed a surge, for the first time in Italy's history, of women writers into the ranks of Italian literary circles. Unlike their counterparts in other countries, such as Britain, France and the United States, this early generation of Italian women writers had little sense of belonging to a female literary tradition. This study has examined the sense of isolation expressed by women writers of the day who, like Neera, regularly encountered negative and derogatory criticism of their work from their male counterparts. In the article "La donna scrittrice," Neera acknowledges the difficulties encountered by women writers and the perseverance required to prevail: "Avete dovuto vincere voi stessa ed altri, sorpassare ostacoli, frangere barriere, prendere sentieri di traverso, per correre ad impugnare la penna che nelle vostre mani significava corruscamento di lama" [You had to conquer yourself and others, overtake obstacles, break barriers, take paths sideways, to run to grab the pen that in your hands meant a shining blade] (*Le idee di una donna* 831–832). She alludes to the woman writer's struggle to succeed as both an internal conflict, overcoming one's own inhibitions to break social barriers by pursuing a profession mainly reserved for men, and an external battle, through the analogy of the pen as a sword in the hands of the woman writer.

In the following excerpt from a letter to literary critic, journalist and poet Giuseppe Saverio Gargàno in 1903, Neera reveals not only the dedication with which she approaches the literary profession but also the sacrifices that it requires of her:

> Ho messo la mia anima, il mio sangue, tutte le paure della mia mesta giovinezza, tutte le aspirazioni della vita nell'arte mia – io ho sdegnato i beni del mondo, il lusso, la gioia, tutto, tutto, per darmi interamente al mio ideale artistico – ho vissuto in un isolamento austero, non ho mai mendicato plausi ed onori, non seguii mai le correnti allettatrici della voga e della moda. *Me stessa* sempre e *sola* sempre andai, andai, andai fissa gli occhi alla meta. La serietà del mio lavoro, comunque sia il merito, anela a un giudizio ugualmente serio. (qtd. Brotto 179)[2]

Neera's efforts and the success she obtained position her within a group of women writers whose endeavors and accomplishments in fin-de-siècle Italian literary circles designate them as literary mothers for later generations of women writers. Sibilla Aleramo, for example, praises Neera's *Teresa* in an article in *La Gazzetta Letteraria* in 1899 as "un capolavoro di analisi e di vero sentimento" [a masterpiece of analysis and true feeling] (qtd. Conti 63) and recognizes Neera as an example "dell'alto valore dell'ingegno muliebre" [of the high value of female ingenuity] (qtd. Conti 68). Feminists of the day also congratulated Neera on *Teresa*, recognizing its importance as a document denouncing female suffering, as emancipationist Ersilia Majno's letter to Neera in 1901 reveals[3]:

> È con profonda commozione ch'io prendo al penna per scriverLe, ... perché Ella sappia che le nostre vie possono ben essere

> diverse, ma che l'autrice di *Teresa* ha e avrà sempre nell'animo d'ogni donna che sente e che pensa un culto d'ammirazione e d'amore. ... Appunto potrà tessere su altro telaio, ma col pensiero comune di dare l'opera nostra per l'elevazione della donna, perché essa possa vivere – a qualunque classe appartenga, colla possibilità di compiere i suoi doveri avendo riconosciuti i suoi diritti da una società oggi troppo ingiusta verso la donna – la madre – la lavoratrice. (qtd. Arslan, *Dame, galline e regine* 140)[4]

Majno notes a common objective shared with Neera: that of working to elevate the female position within a society that is unjust toward women of all social classes and roles. Both Majno and Aleramo acknowledge the importance of Neera's work for the attention it brings to women's oppressed status within society.

Neera's pursual of a career not easily accessible to women at that time, her active role in literary debates and letter exchanges with leading literary, artistic and journalistic figures, her criticism of society's restrictive roles for women and her proposal of the maternal role and instinct as a form of empowerment for women constitute the many and diverse ways in which this fin-de-siècle woman writer rejects contemporary notions of female inferiority and social structures that aim to enforce upon women a model of female submission and passivity. Her multi-faceted persona, as revealed through the multiple voices she adopts in her epistolary exchanges, together with the diverse and at times discrepant positions expressed in the various genres, from literary to theoretical to epistolary, of her production, points to the complexity and determination of this figure as well as to her ability to navigate the intricacies of her profession.

As indicated in the Introduction, the principal goal of this study has been to demonstrate the reasons for bringing Neera out of the condition of literary marginalization to which she has long been unjustly confined. The comprehensive analysis of her vast and varied production offered in the previous chapters serves to locate this writer within the context of Italian literature as a writer who strove constantly for literary innovation, reacting and responding to the literary and social issues and trends of her time. However, perhaps she is best placed inside a matrilineal family tree within the Italian literary landscape, one that recognizes the importance of her legacy as literary mother to the numerous Italian women writers that followed her.

Notes

1 You are not capable of long and severe studies, the scientist told her, and shows her how two and two makes four, that the conformation of her brain, the delicacy of her tissues, the weakness of her fiber, the multiplicity of her needs, reveal that she was not born for science. ... Leave to a mouth less small than yours the difficult articulation of barbaric big words, and do not desire to cloud the smooth marble of your forehead with the wrinkles of calculations, nor to see your heavenly smile among the serious meditations, nor to pale the roses of your face among the prolonged vigils. ... The woman, excluded from knowledge, remained excluded from power; and here she is reduced to absolute passivity, a thing and not being, of greater or lesser relative value, of no intrinsic value, a shadow of all self-consciousness which is the first reason of all strength.

2 I have put my soul, my blood, all the fears of my sad youth, all the aspirations of life into my art – I have disdained the goods of the world, luxury, joy, everything, to give myself entirely to my artistic ideal – I have lived in austere isolation, I have never begged plaudits and honors, I never followed the tantalizing currents of vogue and fashion. I always went by myself alone, with eyes set on the goal. The seriousness of my work, however serious the worth, yearns for an equally serious judgment.

3 Ersilia Majno (1859–1933) was a prominent activist for the Italian women's movement. She served as president of the *Associazione Generale delle Operaie*, founder of the journal *Unione femminile* and founder and director for approximately ten years of the *Unione Femminile* association.

4 It is with deep emotion that I take the pen to write you, ... so that you know that our ways may well be different, but that *Teresa*'s author has and will always have in the soul of every woman who feels and thinks a cult of admiration and love. ... You might weave on another loom, but with the common thought of giving our work for the elevation of woman, so that she can live – whatever class she belongs to, with the possibility of fulfilling her duties, having recognized her rights from a society that today is too unfair to woman – the mother – the worker.

References

Brotto, Manuela. "Un'artista e lo specchio della critica. Il carteggio inedito tra Neera e Gargàno." *Cuadernos de Filologia Italiana*, vol. 8, 2001, pp. 165–183.

Conti, Bruna, editori. *Sibilla Aleramo. La donna e il femminismo.* Rome, Riuniti, 1978.

Neera. *Le idee di una donna.* 1903. *Neera*, edited by Benedetto Croce, Milano, Garzanti, 1942, pp. 777–867.

Pieroni Bortolotti, Franca. *Alle origini del movimento femminile in Italia. 1848–1892.* Turin, Einaudi, 1963.

Index

Note: Page numbers followed by "n" denote endnotes.

Zeitfracht Medien GmbH
Ferdinand-Jühlke-Straße 7
99095 Erfurt, Deutschland
produktsicherheit@kolibri360.de